On Deck

USS LEXINGTON (CV-16)

By Al Adcock
Color by Don Greer
Illustrated by John Lowe

On Deck Number 2

squadron/signal publications

Introduction

The aircraft carrier **USS LEXINGTON** (CV-2) sank at the Battle of the Coral Sea on 8 May 1942. The same day, workers 8000 miles (12,874.4 км) away were constructing the ESSEX class carrier USS CABOT (CV-16). This ship was laid down at Bethlehem Steel's Fore River Shipyards in Quincy, Massachusetts on 15 September 1941. The workers soon heard of LEXINGTON's sinking and sent a telegram to Secretary of the Navy Frank Knox. The workers asked Knox to change the new ship's name from CABOT to LEXINGTON. Knox replied the same day and authorized the renaming of this carrier. Superhuman efforts resulted in the launching of LEXINGTON (CV-16) on 26 September 1942 and its commissioning on 17 February 1943 – fully one year ahead of schedule. This accelerated schedule meant that LEXINGTON could soon take the fight to the Japanese and avenge her namesake's loss.

LEXINGTON stood out for a shakedown cruise to the Caribbean Sea following her commissioning. She was painted in the Measure 21 Navy Blue System, which she wore for much of her wartime service. By May of 1943, the carrier began embarking Carrier Air Group Sixteen (CVG-16), which included Grumman F4F-4 Wildcat fighters, Douglas SBD-4 Dauntless dive-bombers, and Grumman TBF-1 Avenger torpedo-bombers. The Air Group soon exchanged their Wildcats for Grumman F6F-3 Hellcats, which were faster and better armed and armored than the earlier F4Fs. LEXINGTON completed her shakedown cruise and passed through the Panama Canal into the Pacific Ocean and the war zone.

Her first action occurred from 11 to 23 September 1943, when her aircraft raided Tarawa Atoll in the Gilbert Islands. LEXINGTON launched air attacks on Wake Island in October, then raided Tarawa and Kwajalein in the Marshalls the following month. The carrier was first damaged by enemy action on the night of 4 December, when Japanese Mitsubishi G4M1 torpedo-bombers (Allied codename Betty) attacked her off Kwajalein. One torpedo hit LEXINGTON's starboard fantail area, which jammed her rudder and caused her to circle uncontrollably to port. Steering repairs were made overnight, but the carrier was out of action. The attack killed nine crewmen and injured 35 others. Infamous radio propaganda commentator 'Tokyo Rose' claimed that Japanese forces sank LEXINGTON.

The carrier was repaired and refitted at Pearl Harbor, Hawaii before attacking Mille Atoll in the Marshall Islands on 18 March 1944. This reappearance prompted 'Tokyo Rose' to nickname LEXINGTON the 'Blue Ghost.' She would announce the carrier's 'sinking' three more times during the war. LEXINGTON's F6Fs shot down 45 Japanese aircraft during the Battle of the Philippine Sea ('The Great Marianas Turkey Shoot') in June of 1944.

LEXINGTON was the target of a Japanese *kamikaze* ('Divine Wind') suicide attack off Luzon in the Philippines on 5 November 1944. A Mitsubishi A6M5 Zero fighter (Allied codename Zeke) circled around her stern and crashed high on the island superstructure's starboard side. The impact rained metal and burning gasoline onto the 20MM gallery, killing 50 sailors and wounding 130 others. Despite this, LEXINGTON's gunners downed another Zero which was attacking her sister ship, USS TICONDEROGA (CV-14).

LEXINGTON was placed in the Reserve Fleet at Bremerton, Washington in 1947. In 1953, she was recalled, recommissioned, and modernized with an angled flight deck and modified island. LEXINGTON was redesignated CVA-16 on her recommissioning on 15 August 1955, when she joined the Seventh Fleet in the Pacific. Redesignated CVS-16 on 1 October 1962, she was selected to replace USS ANTIETAM (CV-36) as the US Navy's training carrier. LEXINGTON was transferred to Pensacola, Florida and assumed these duties on 20 December 1962. Her designation was changed to CVT-16 on 16 January 1969 and to AVT-16 on 1 July 1978. The carrier served in the training role until her decommissioning on 26 November 1991. LEXINGTON was towed to her present site in Corpus Christi, Texas following her decommissioning and is now a museum ship open to the public.

Acknowledgements

Judith Whipple, Curator, USS LEXINGTON
  Museum on the Bay
Col Earl M. Chu, USAF (Ret.)
Cdr Mike Sablowski, USN (Ret.)
Cdr Doug Seigfried, USN (Ret)
Commodore Marty Morgan, USN
The Hook (Tailhook Association magazine)
United States Naval Institute (USNI)
Elsilrac Enterprises, Bob Carlisle

Real War Photos, George Chizmar
Floating Drydock, Tom Walkowiak
US Navy
Pat Nichols
NAS Pensacola Public Affairs Office
Grumman, Roger Seybel
Hill Goodspeed, National Museum of Naval
  Aviation (NMNA)
Frank Taunton
Jim Adcock

ISBN 0-89747-449-X

If you have any photographs of aircraft, armor, soldiers or ships of any nation, particularly wartime snapshots, why not share them with us and help make Squadron/Signal's books all the more interesting and complete in the future. Any photograph sent to us will be copied and the original returned. The donor will be fully credited for any photos used. Please send them to:

Squadron/Signal Publications, Inc.
1115 Crowley Drive
Carrollton, TX 75011-5010

Если у вас есть фотографии самолётов, вооружения, солдат или кораблей любой страны, особенно, снимки времён войны, поделитесь с нами и помогите сделать новые книги издательства Эскадрон/Сигнал ещё интереснее. Мы переснимем ваши фотографии и вернём оригиналы. Имена приславших снимки будут сопровождать все опубликованные фотографии. Пожалуйста, присылайте фотографии по адресу:

Squadron/Signal Publications, Inc.
1115 Crowley Drive
Carrollton, TX 75011-5010

軍用機、装甲車両、兵士、軍艦などの写真を所持しておられる方はいらっしゃいませんか？どの国のものでも結構です。作戦中に撮影されたものが特に良いのです。Squadron/Signal社の出版する刊行物において、このような写真は内容を一層充実し、興味深くすることができます。当方にお送り頂いた写真は、複写の後お返しいたします。出版物中に写真を使用した場合は、必ず提供者のお名前を明記させて頂きます。お写真は下記にご送付ください。

Squadron/Signal Publications, Inc.
1115 Crowley Drive
Carrollton, TX 75011-5010

(Front Cover) An Eastern Aircraft TBM-1C Avenger from Torpedo Squadron Twenty (VT-20) makes its final approach for landing on USS LEXINGTON (CV-16) in December of 1944, following a raid on shipping in the Formosa Strait. LEXINGTON is painted in Measure 21, the Navy Blue System, which she had for most of her wartime career.

(Previous Page) USS LEXINGTON (CV-16) sails in the Pacific Ocean in 1943 just prior to the raids on the Marshall and Gilbert Islands. She is camouflaged in Measure 21, the Navy Blue System that earned her the nickname of 'Blue Ghost.' LEXINGTON's crew called her the 'Fighting Lady,' because she saw action from Tarawa in 1943 to Tokyo Bay in 1945. (USNI)

(Back Cover) Two McDonnell Douglas TA-4J Skyhawks fly over LEXINGTON (AVT-16) in September of 1988. Other Skyhawks are spotted on her flight deck. Over 42,000 Naval aviators were carrier qualified on LEXINGTON. The 'Blue Ghost' served as the US Navy's only training carrier from 1962 until she was decommissioned in 1991.

USS LEXINGTON (CV-2) stands out in Pensacola Bay, Florida before the start of World War Two. The boat booms are extended to facilitate the embarking crew. The stern landing ramp was designed to aid in a low approach landing and to protect the carrier's stern. (US Navy)

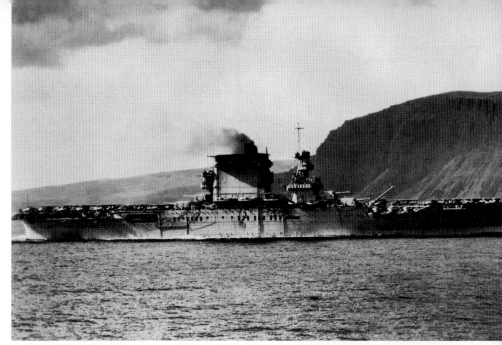

LEXINGTON sails into Pearl Harbor, Hawaii in the early 1930s. She and her sister SARATOGA (CV-3) were converted from battle cruisers to aircraft carriers to comply with the Washington Naval Treaty of 1922. The deck is covered with Boeing F4B and Grumman FF fighters. (US Navy)

LEXINGTON burns after being attacked by Japanese aircraft during the Battle of the Coral Sea on 8 May 1942. The damage inflicted by the Japanese was greater than the carrier's damage control parties could handle. This situation resulted in LEXINGTON's crew abandoning the ship. A US Navy destroyer fired torpedoes to sink LEXINGTON, which prevented her from falling into enemy hands. (US Navy)

The ESSEX class carrier LEXINGTON (CV-16) is launched from Bethlehem Steel's Fore River Shipyard in Quincy, Massachusetts on 26 September 1942. This occurred just over one year after she was laid down as USS CABOT (CV-16) on 15 September 1941. Her name was changed to commemorate the carrier USS LEXINGTON (CV-2), which was lost during the Battle of the Coral Sea. The island superstructure and other items were installed after LEXINGTON was launched. She was the eighth of 26 ESSEX class carriers ordered between 1940 and 1943. LEXINGTON was the second of these ships to be commissioned; class leader ESSEX (CV-9) joined the fleet on 31 December 1942. (National Archives)

LEXINGTON rests at her final mooring on Corpus Christi Bay in Corpus Christi, Texas in 1999. She was decommissioned at Pensacola, Florida on 26 November 1991. LEXINGTON was towed from Pensacola to Corpus Christi in 1992 and was opened to the public as a museum on 14 October 1992. The non-profit USS LEXINGTON Museum on the Bay oper- ates the 'LEX' today. She is painted in the Measure 27 system of Haze Gray (5-H, approx- imately FS35237). The boot topping immediately above the waterline is black; this color was meant to hide oil stains in the water. (Carol Adcock)

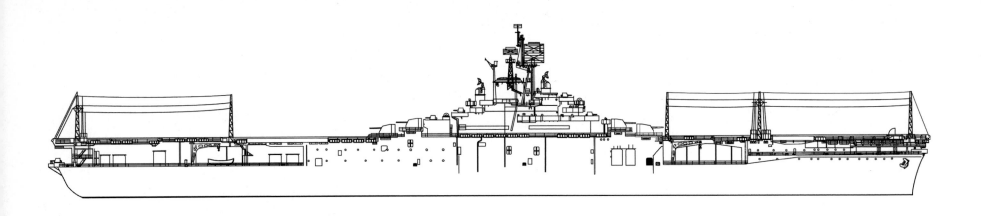

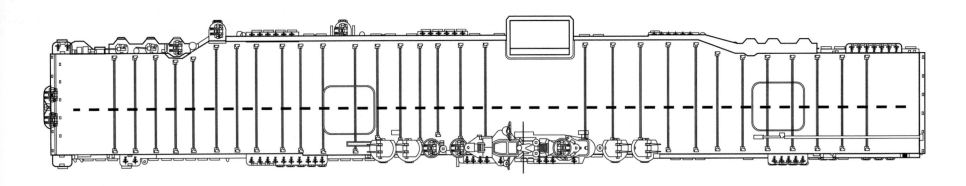

USS LEXINGTON (CV-16) Specifications (1945)

Length (Overall):.872 feet (265.8 M)

Beam:...................147 feet 6 inches (45 M)

Draft:......................27 feet 6 inches (8.4 M)

Displacement:.......27,200 tons (24,675.8 MT) Standard, 34,880 tons (31,643.1 MT) Full Load

Propulsion:...........150,000 SHP/Four Screws

Speed:..................33 knots (38 MPH/61.2 KMH)

Range:..................15,000 NM (17,272.7 miles/27,797 KM) at 15 knots (17.3 MPH/27.8 KMH)

Complement:.......275 Officers and 2365 Enlisted Men

Armament:............12 x 5 Inch (12.7 CM)/38 Calibre Guns in Four Twin Turrets and Four Single Mounts, 64 x 40MM Bofors Cannon in 14 Quad Mounts, 60 x 20MM Oerlikon Cannon in 30 Twin Mounts, and 20 x .50 Calibre (12.7MM) Browning Machine Guns in 5 Quad Mounts.

Total Aircraft:......103, Including: 31 F6F Hellcat fighters, 4 Hellcat night fighters, 2 Hellcat reconnaissance aircraft, 36 F4U Corsair fighters, 15 SB2C Helldiver dive-bombers, and 15 TBM Avenger torpedo-bombers

(Right) LEXINGTON conducts sea trials in the Atlantic Ocean off Boston, Massachusetts in early 1943. She is painted in Measure 21, the Navy Blue System. The vertical surfaces above the waterline were painted Navy Blue (5-N, approximately FS35044). Metal horizontal surfaces were Deck Blue (20-B, approximately FS35042), while the wooden flight deck was stained Blue Flight Deck Stain 21 – nearly identical to 20-B. Paint along the hull is already weathered from exposure to the sea's harsh conditions. Various radar antennas are mounted on the island. The lattice radio masts along her flight deck are lowered for flight operations. (Real War Photos)

(Below) A supply ship steams off LEXINGTON's starboard side during the carrier's shakedown cruise in early 1943. LEXINGTON is armed with the new 40mm Bofors anti-aircraft guns in gun tubs located at her stern and along the flight deck. Galleries for 20mm Oerlikon cannon are located along the flight deck sides. Upon completion of her trials, LEXINGTON was commissioned on 17 February 1943. (Real War Photos)

LEXINGTON is viewed from the flight deck of a Grumman C-1A Trader Carrier Onboard Delivery (COD) aircraft. The COD's pilot has just turned onto final approach from the downwind leg. He soon acquires the Optical Landing System (OLS), also called the 'ball,' to determine if the deck is safe to recover aboard. (Al Adcock)

The horizontal green lights on the OLS bar indicate to the pilot that he is properly aligned with the deck and will catch the number 3 arresting cable ('wire'). The pilot is in contact with the Landing Signal Officer (LSO) near the OLS and the Carrier Air Traffic Control Center (CATCC) while approaching LEXINGTON. (Al Adcock)

The C-1A is on final approach to LEXINGTON and is in the 'groove' for a smooth recovery. Green lights lit on the 'ball' indicate a clear deck. The C-1A is approximately one quarter mile (0.4 KM) from touchdown. The nylon cord on the windshield's port side indicated wind shear during flight. The Trader's tail hook, landing gear, and flaps are lowered and it is cleared to land. (Al Adcock)

The C-1A is now 200 feet (61 M) up and one eighth of a mile (0.2 KM) out as the final approach is made to LEXINGTON. The dark spot on the landing area is the location of the four arresting cables, or 'wires.' The 'ball' is set to guide the aircraft to the number 3 cable, the most desired landing situation. (Al Adcock)

Three deck crewmen near the island watch the C-1A taxi past soon after landing. Their helmets have ear covers to protect against the high noise levels on the flight deck, while tinted goggles protect their eyes from sunlight and foreign objects in the air. White dots on the flight deck are pad eyes used to chain aircraft down to the deck. (Al Adcock)

The COD is almost over the ramp, with green lights on the 'ball' and seconds away from touchdown. The LSO stands on the deck, out of the cover of his platform to get a better view of the landing aircraft. All landings are televised to LEXINGTON's Captain, the Air Boss, and the ready rooms. (Al Adcock)

The C-1A COD taxis towards LEXINGTON's starboard bow catapult, prior to launch. One of the yellow-shirted aircraft handling officers stands near the catapult to guide the aircraft. Catapult crewmen in green shirts prepare the catapult for launching the Trader. (Al Adcock)

LEXINGTON steams through ice-filled Boston Harbor soon after her commissioning on 17 February 1943. Her deck-edge radio masts are raised and her forward elevator is lowered. The port deck edge elevator folded 90° to ease the ship's passage through the Panama Canal. (US Navy)

LEXINGTON cruises off the US West Coast on 20 February 1944. The carrier left Puget Sound Navy Yard in Bremerton, Washington that day for San Francisco after repairs and refitting. The radio antenna towers are in the upright position. Galleries for 20MM cannon are located along the flight deck edges, while side hull sponsons held 40MM cannon. (Real War Photos)

The number two deck elevator is lowered to LEXINGTON's hangar deck in 1944. The ship's pennant number (16) and the dashed lines are black on the Deck Blue stained flight deck. LEXINGTON had 11 arresting cables across her aft flight deck during this period. She was originally fitted with one catapult, but the number two (port) catapult was added in early 1944. LEXINGTON did not receive the hangar deck catapult fitted to the first five ESSEX class carriers. (Floating Drydock)

LEXINGTON sails for the Central Pacific with Carrier Air Group Sixteen (CVG-16) embarked in April of 1943. CVG-16 comprised the Grumman F6F-3 Hellcats of Fighting Squadron Sixteen (VF-16), the Douglas SBD-4 Dauntlesses of Bombing Squadrons Sixteen and Twenty Three (VB-16 and VB-23), and the Grumman TBF-1 Avengers of Torpedo Squadron Sixteen (VT-16). The SBDs spotted on the aft flight deck are painted in a combination of the older Blue Gray (FS35189) over Light Gray (FS36493) and the new tri-color camouflage schemes. The latter scheme consisted of Sea Blue (FS35045) upper surfaces, Intermediate Blue (FS35164) sides, and flat White (FS37875) undersurfaces. LEXINGTON does not have her side mounted 40MM anti-aircraft guns fitted at this time. (Floating Drydock)

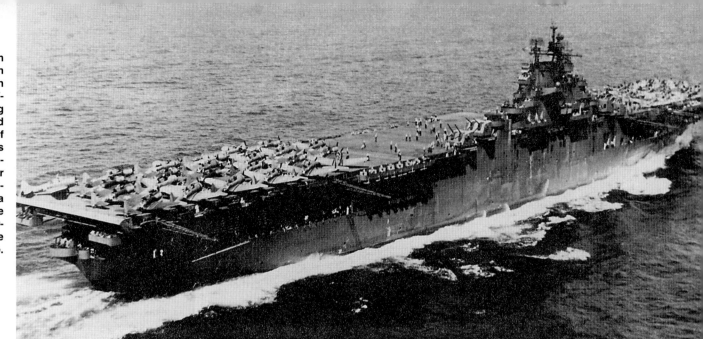

A VF-16 F6F-3 Hellcat taxis forward on LEXINGTON's flight deck in September of 1943. Eleven TBF-1s from VT-16 are spotted at the bow, with their wings folded to increase space on the crowded flight and hangar decks. Aircraft from CVG-16 raided Tarawa Atoll in the Gilbert Islands from 11 to 23 September. This series of attacks marked LEXINGTON's first combat action. US Marines invaded Tarawa on 23 November 1943, capturing the atoll after heavy fighting three days later. (Real War Photos)

A yellow-shirted plane director guides a VF-16 F6F-3 forward on LEXINGTON's flight deck in 1944. The Hellcat has crossed the second row of cable crash barriers raised to stop aircraft that unsuccessfully engage the arresting cables. The Deck Blue stain is worn on sections of the wooden flight deck. (National Archives)

The catapult officer, or 'shooter,' in the yellow jersey readies a TA-4J from Training Squadron Twenty One (VT-21) on LEXINGTON's number one catapult. When he places his finger on the deck, an operator on the starboard deck edge launches the Skyhawk. The green shirt to starboard of the 'shooter' monitors the catapult pressure gauges. (Art Giberson)

Purple shirted refueling crews, nicknamed 'grapes,' refuel a Douglas TA-4J Skyhawk aboard LEXINGTON. They pump fuel using the aircraft's in-flight refueling probe. The 500 painted on the deck indicates the number of feet from the bow. A non-skid coating was applied over LEXINGTON's wooden flight deck, which gives the illusion of a painted steel surface. (Al Adcock)

Flight Deck Crew Jerseys

Blue

Worn by Aircraft Handlers & Tractor Drivers (with Blue Helmet), Elevator Operators (with White Helmet), and by Aircraft Directors (with Yellow Helmet)

Brown

Worn by Plane Captains (with Brown Helmet) and by Helicopter Plane Captains (with Red Helmet)

Green

Worn by Arresting/Catapult Crew (with Green Helmet), by Arresting/Catapult Officers (with Yellow Helmet), and by Replenishment Officers (with White Helmet)

A squadron plane inspector in his black and white checkered 'float coat' (survival vest) checks the port flaps of a Grumman A-6E Intruder in September of 1988. The A-6E was assigned to Attack Squadron One Twenty Eight (VA-128) 'Golden Eagles,' which was the Intruder West Coast Replacement Air Group (RAG). VA-128 deployed aboard LEXINGTON for carrier requalifications. (Al Adcock)

Purple

Worn by Refuelers (with Purple Helmets)

Red

Worn by Ordnance/Crash Crew (with Red Helmets)

White

Worn by Safety/Medical/Transfer Crew (with White Helmets), by Landing Signals Officers (with No Helmet), and by Plane Inspectors (with Green Helmets)

Yellow

Worn by Plane Directors/Landing Officers (with Yellow Helmets) and Catapult and Arresting Gear Crew (with Green Helmets)

A brown shirt plane captain confers with the bombardier/navigator of a VA-128 A-6E in September of 1988. The distinct colors of the deck crews' jerseys, helmets, and vests ease their identification to the Air Boss and to their crewmates. The Squadron had flown from Naval Air Station (NAS) Whidbey Island, Washington to conduct annual carrier qualifications aboard LEXINGTON in the Gulf of Mexico. (Al Adcock)

A Japanese torpedo aircraft hit by LEXINGTON's anti-aircraft gunners crashes into the Pacific on 4 December 1943. This aircraft was the third shot down that day by the carrier's gunners, while she operated off the Marshall Islands. Dark smoke puffs from exploding anti-aircraft shells fill the sky around LEXINGTON and an escorting ship in the distance. By the end of World War Two, LEXINGTON's gunners shot down 17 Japanese aircraft. (Real War Photos)

LEXINGTON rests near Puget Sound Navy Yard on 16 February 1944. The carrier was at the Bremerton, Washington facility for repairs after the 4 December 1943 attack off Kwajalein. During wartime, the Navy brought in warships to upgrade and repair equipment, including electronics and machinery. The ship also received a fresh coat of paint and new crewmembers. The Carrier Air Group was working up at its shore base while the carrier was at the yard. (Floating Drydock)

On 5 November 1944, a Japanese naval pilot crashed his Mitsubishi A6M Zero into LEXINGTON's starboard island. This *kamikaze* ('Divine Wind') suicide attack occurred while the carrier operated off Luzon in the Philippine Islands. The attack killed the pilot and 50 American sailors, while another 130 crewmen were wounded. This marked the second time enemy action caused major damage to LEXINGTON and she soon steamed to Ulithi in the Carolines for repairs.

LEXINGTON underwent her final wartime refit at Bremerton from March until May of 1945. This refit included a repainting in the Measure 12 scheme, which was a modified Graded System of Ocean Gray (5-O, approximately FS35164) and Sea Blue (5-S, approximately FS35045). LEXINGTON was previously painted in the Measure 21 Navy Blue System. This scheme and her erroneously reported sinkings earned LEXINGTON her nickname of the 'Blue Ghost.' (Real War Photos)

15

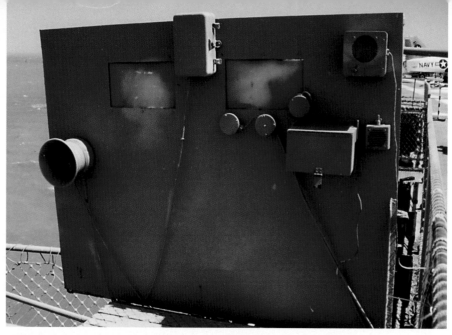

This Landing Signal Officer (LSO) wears a jump suit with brightly colored red and yellow striping during the early 1950s. The outfit was intended to make him more visible to incoming pilots. Early LSOs used brightly colored table tennis paddles to direct pilots, who nicknamed the LSOs 'paddles.' This LSO uses paddles with bright cloth strips. A clear view port was added to the canvas windscreen aft of the LSO in 1945. (Elsilrac)

LEXINGTON's LSO was stationed on the opposite side of this screen along the flight deck. Speakers mounted on the screen relayed information from Primary Flight Control (Pri-Fly) on the island and from landing aircraft. This sheet metal screen replaced the earlier canvas windscreen by 1976. The two clear view ports were slightly enlarged in 1988 over those ports originally fitted. (Al Adcock)

1943-45 LSO Windscreen

The LSO's screen was erected to shield the LSO from Wind Over the Deck (WOD) and from weather coming from the bow. Escape netting under this shield was installed to allow the LSO to escape from the flight deck in the event of a bad approach. (Al Adcock)

A plastic weather protection cover is placed over LEXINGTON's Optical Landing System (OLS, or 'meatball') in 1999. The OLS consists of green, yellow, and red lights illuminated to inform approaching pilots of deck conditions and his attitude and altitude for final approach. A green light with a yellow center light indicates a correct approach, while a red light tells the pilot the deck is fouled or the approach is too high or too low. (Al Adcock)

A fairlead sheave connects each end of the arresting cable across the flight deck. The sheaves guide the cable from the flight deck to the arresting engine below deck. Pri-Fly adjusted the cable's tension according to the landing aircraft's weight. LEXINGTON could handle aircraft with gross weights up to 70,000 pounds (31,752 KG). The largest and heaviest aircraft to fly off this ship was the Douglas A3D (later A-3) Skywarrior. (Al Adcock)

The OLS mounted on LEXINGTON is also called a Fresnel lens, after the French design it was based on. Pri-Fly set the lens to coincide with the aircraft's optimum angle of attack so that it would catch ('hook') the Number Three arresting cable ('wire'). The OLS compensated for the angle of the deck and the carrier's speed. (NMNA)

The wire terminal sheaves on the starboard side are designed for wheels to roll over it while the ones on the port side are not. The ones on the starboard side are in the area of the 'junk yard,' the deck storage area for the crash recover crane ('tilly'), along with fork lifts and tugs. (Al Adcock)

17

An LSO brings home one of his squadron's aircraft in 1945, while all eyes are on the approaching aircraft. Each squadron had their own LSO, who knew each pilot for whom he was responsible for getting safely back on the deck. Late in World War Two, a square view port was added to the plain canvas LSO screen. (Elsilrac)

A VF-16 F6F-3 Hellcat from VF-16 revs its engine to full power before launching from LEXINGTON in 1943. The aircraft used approximately half of the 862 foot (262.7 M) long flight deck to get airborne without using the ship's catapult. Several SBD-5 Dauntless await their turn to launch, while a SOUTH DAKOTA class battleship trails LEXINGTON to port. (US Navy)

An LSO has given the 'cut' sign to the pilot of a Douglas SBD-4 of VB-16 as he comes aboard in April of 1943. This recovery occurred during LEXINGTON's shakedown cruise in the Caribbean following her commissioning on 17 February. Two LSOs are on duty at all times during flight operations, allowing one to take over in case the other became incapacitated. (Elsilrac)

Aircraft machinist's mates bring 130 gallon (492.1 L) fuel tanks out to VB-19's Curtiss SB2C-3 Helldivers spotted on LEXINGTON's aft flight deck on 25 October 1944. The tanks were installed in the bomb bay to extend its range for a mission to locate the Japanese fleet. The Helldiver was often called upon to become a scout bomber, a role for which it was not suited. (Elsilrac)

Pilots and radio operator/gunners begin leaving their SBD-5s on the forward flight deck to the charge of the plane captains. The Dauntlesses had just returned from raiding Tarawa on 18 September 1943. Air Intelligence Officers are making their initial inquiries of the pilots and crews regarding the conditions over the target, while the medical staff is checking for injuries. (Real War Photo)

A yellow-shirted plane director brings an F6F-3 Hellcat from VF-16 up to take off position on 19 November 1943. The Hellcat was launched from LEXINGTON for the first raid on Mille Atoll in the Marshall Islands. The Hellcat was armed with six wing-mounted .50 caliber (12.7MM) machine guns and had a top speed of 380 MPH (611.5 KMH). (US Navy)

A North American T-2C Buckeye from VT-4 makes an arrested landing on LEXINGTON. The arms at left belong to a lookout with binoculars searching for civilian boats that may be cruising near the carrier. Repairs, patching, and resurfacing with anti-skid/sealer coat-ings resulted in the various flight deck colors late in LEXINGTON's career. The LSO and his assistant stand on the flight deck edge, out from behind their screen, while the T-2C 'traps' aboard the ship. (Al Adcock)

A Grumman A-6E Intruder taxis to starboard for turning while another A-6E makes a landing approach over the ramp. It was necessary to turn the large A-6 on the elevator, since there was not enough room on the flight deck to do so during flight operations. The yellow recovery crane 'tilly' is located on the starboard side of the 'junk yard.' (Al Adcock)

One of LEXINGTON's Mk 11 motor whaleboats is located on the carrier's starboard side athwartships (across from) the deck edge elevator. This 26 foot (7.9 M) long vessel could carry up to 24 men and was designed for hoisting by either davits or a sling. The whaleboat was used to transport personnel to shore, another ship, or for evacuation during an emergency aboard the carrier. (Al Adcock)

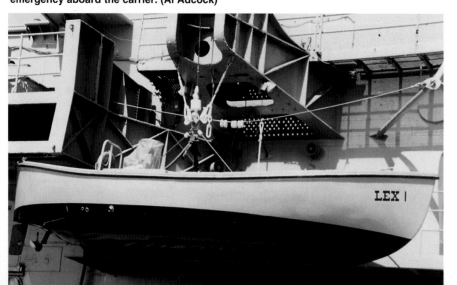

A 1942 model aircraft tug is displayed aboard LEXINGTON at Corpus Christi. It had pintle hooks on the front and rear to engage tow bars. The bars were connected to the aircraft for positioning on the flight and hangar decks. This tug undergoing restoration was painted in gray primer and was later painted in Orange Yellow (FS13538). (Al Adcock)

A gray flight deck tractor heads past SBD-5s of VB-16 aboard LEXINGTON during the Gilberts Operation in November of 1943. One crewman drives the vehicle, while another stands behind the driver. This tractor was on its way to help respot another aircraft on deck. The US Navy modified farm vehicles into aircraft tractors during World War Two. (Cdr Edward Steichen, US Navy)

LEXINGTON was equipped with a mobile LeTorneau aircraft recovery crane, better known as 'tilly.' It was used to recover disabled aircraft on deck and to lift heavy objects. In the event of a deck crash, it would be necessary for 'tilly' to remove the aircraft as soon as possible so flight operations could resume. (Al Adcock)

An A-6E Intruder reaches the end of the catapult track and is about to become airborne from LEXINGTON. The A-6 was pulled along the catapult track by a launch bar attached to the nose landing gear. The Intruder reached an airspeed of 120 knots (138.2 MPH/222.4 KMH) at the end of the catapult track. (Al Adcock)

The A-6E has left the deck while another A-6 makes a pass down the port side following a wave off. The Intruder served with US Navy and Marine operational squadrons until replaced by the McDonnell Douglas (now Boeing) F/A-18 Hornet in the mid-1990s. (Al Adcock)

An A-6E undergoes a preflight check on LEXINGTON's Number One catapult prior to launch. The Jet Blast Deflector (JBD) is extended just prior to launch. The JBD is lowered once the Intruder is launched to allow the next aircraft to taxi over it and onto the catapult track. (Al Adcock)

Jet Blast Deflector Development

1957 (Single Panel)

1988 (Three-Panel)

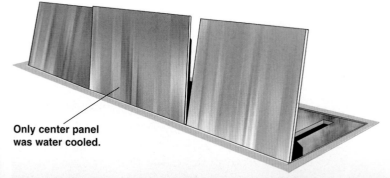

Only center panel
was water cooled.

An A-6E from VA-128 comes in over LEXINGTON's ramp in 1988. VA-128 had flown in that day from NAS Whidbey Island on a cross-country flight, making aerial refueling hook-ups on the way. The Intruder's ailerons split to form speedbrakes on landing to help slow down the aircraft. (Al Adcock)

An electronics mate points the AN/SPN-44 Doppler radar at an A-6E that just landed and engaged the number four 'wire.' The Doppler radar was used to determine the touchdown speed of landing aircraft. The large dome to port housed the AN/SPN-35 approach radar, which provided glide slope information to aircraft during inclement weather. (Al Adcock)

This VA-128 A-6E has just engaged the preferred number three cable and touched down on the landing area centerline. It will soon be dragged to a stop after this near perfect recovery. The hook runner coming from off the starboard wing soon disengaged the wire from the hook before the A-6 was directed to a parking area. (Al Adcock)

This A-6E has caught the number one 'wire,' which indicated a too low and too fast approach. It can be assured that the Air-Boss will have a few choice words with the pilot – the Air-Boss talking and the pilot listening. The camera operator located just under Pri-Fly televised the landing for evaluation purposes. (Al Adcock)

Two VT-4 T-2C Buckeyes are lined up behind LEXINGTON's Number One catapult JBD in the area called 'the street.' The yellow outline for the Number Two catapult JBD is located just behind the tail of T-2C number 00. Deck checkers stand on the starboard side foul line (striped yellow and red) for the landing area. (Al Adcock)

The Number One catapult control station is located on the starboard flight deck edge. This position is manned by a deck edge catapult operator wearing a green shirt, who actually 'fires' the catapult on the Catapult Officer's command. The launch signal is the Catapult Officer touching his finger to the deck. (Al Adcock)

A TA-4J Skyhawk is pulled down the catapult track while another waits its turn behind the protection of the Jet Blast Deflector (JBD). The JBD is deployed to direct the jet blast over the island and not along the deck. The jet exhaust produces over 1000° Fahrenheit (537.8° Celsius) temperatures at a velocity exceeding 1160 MPH (1866.8 KMH). Many an unsuspecting deck crewman has been injured or – worst yet – blown overboard by the exhaust effects. (Al Adcock)

The Center Deck Operator (CDO) mans his position between the two catapults. He communicates with catapult control by relaying the type, gross weight, and side number of the aircraft on the catapult. The CDO also assists in selecting the Capacity Selector Valve (CSV) setting for the steam catapult. Various launch bridles are located adjacent to his position. The 2 painted on the deck indicates this is the second of four helicopter tie down spots. (Al Adcock)

Tools of the catapult crew's trade are laid out between LEXINGTON's two catapults. Various adapters and bridles are being positioned between the red and white foul lines. Each bridle weighs approximately 120 pounds (54.4 KG). The TA-4J/M, C-1A, and the T-2C required bridles to connect the aircraft to the catapult. The A-6 was fitted with a catapult tow bar, which was mounted on the nose landing gear. (Al Adcock)

A white and red fire truck is positioned between the white deck centerline and the landing area foul line, while a TA-4J is positioned on the starboard catapult. The white shirted safety crew observes the deck and watches the foul line, which marks the landing area's outer border. A yellow E is painted on the deck as a self-proclaimed efficiency award for the catapults. The catapult crew has arrayed the bridles and adapters for various aircraft between the E and the CDO's station. A red and yellow striped border is painted around the aircraft elevator. (Al Adcock)

(Above Left) A North American FJ-3M Fury goes down LEXINGTON's Number One elevator while another FJ-3 (D-102) from VF-121 'Pacesetters' is prepared for launch. Catapult crewmen return bridles from the forward flight deck to the launch area. The bridle was released from the aircraft when it reached the end of the flight deck and was caught by the bridle arrestor at the bow. Various types of the FJ-3 Fury served on LEXINGTON from 1957 until 1962. The Fury was a navalized version of the US Air Force's F-86 Sabre. (The Hook)

(Above) A T-2C Buckeye's pilot advances his throttles to full power prior to the Catapult Officer giving the launch signal. The Center Deck Operator (CDO) sitting nearby orders the proper steam pressure for the catapult to launch the Buckeye. The T-2C was assigned to VT-23 'Professionals' from NAS Kingsville, Texas, just outside Corpus Christi. The US Navy used the Buckeye to train selected students in advanced air-to-air combat. In 1959, the Buckeye entered US Navy service as the T2J-1 (redesignated T-2A in 1962). The T-2C first flew in 1968 and served in US Navy training squadrons until replaced by the Boeing (formerly McDonnell Douglas) T-45 Goshawk in the early 1990s.

(Left) A blue shirted aircraft handler prepares his chains to secure an aircraft to LEXINGTON's deck. The wheel chock placed immediately to starboard of him prevents aircraft movement on deck. The 'Blue Shirts,' also called the 'chain gang,' were also responsible for the handling equipment, including tractors and aircraft starting units. A TA-4J (A-742) is prepared for launch in the background. The catapult crew needs to fit a bridle from the catapult to the aircraft and install a hold back bar before launching. The hold back bar secures the aircraft to a cleat located at the catapult's aft end until launch, when it breaks off and allows the aircraft to move forward. (US Navy)

(Above) The 'Shooter' (Catapult Officer) watches while a TA-4J (A-723) from VT-7 moves down LEXINGTON's 211 foot (64.3 M) long catapult track. The C-11 catapult is powered by steam from the ship's boilers and could launch aircraft weighing up to 70,000 pounds (31,752 KG). LEXINGTON was fitted with two C-11s when she was modernized from 1953 to 1955. These replaced the carrier's original H-4 hydraulic catapults, which were less effective in launching jet aircraft. Launch bridles are placed to port of the Catapult Officer. (US Navy)

(Above Right) The Deck Edge Operator, standing with arms raised in the starboard sponson, prepares to launch a TA-4J (A-735) from LEXINGTON's Number One catapult. At the end of the catapult track, a rope catcher keeps the bridle from going into the water. The words CAT GRIP painted on the Center Deck Operator's position hatch reminds the pilot to grip the 'cat grip' bar just forward of the throttle. This bar prevents the pilot from grabbing the throttle and pulling it back towards the idle position, due to the sudden acceleration of the catapult launch. (US Navy)

(Right) An A-6E Intruder (AD-503) from VA-42 'Green Pawns' awaits the Catapult Officer's launch signal. VA-42 was operating as the East Coast Replacement Air Group (RAG) for A-6 squadrons while they conducted Carrier Qualifications onboard LEXINGTON. The Squadron flew from its home base of NAS Oceana, Virginia to the carrier. The Center Deck Operator mans his position in the chair aft of the Catapult Officer. (Elsilrac)

The forward part of LEXINGTON's island contains the Navigation Bridge, with the Flag Bridge below it. Atop the Navigation Bridge is a civilian radar antenna for the Pathfinder radar set. Immediately behind the Pathfinder radar is a companion search radar, which occupies the former position of the post Korean War era Mk 25 gun director. LEXINGTON's island was extensively remodeled during her refit of 1953 to 1955. (Al Adcock)

The naval aviation insignia – blue anchors and yellow wings – is painted on the front of LEXINGTON's island. The preservation committee decided to repaint this area Haze Gray (5-H) for appearance sake. The lower island was painted black during her training carrier service to hide aircraft exhaust stains. (Al Adcock)

A flight deck extension was fitted around the starboard side of the island. This extension was added during her early 1950s modernization and allowed passage around the island without interfering with flight deck operations. The red E painted above the hull number 16 indicated engineering excellence. The ship's navigator was positioned in the bridge wing behind the navigation bridge. (Al Adcock)

LEXINGTON's 'fruit salad' of 12 ribbons on her starboard island side represent awards she earned in the Pacific during World War Two. The ribbons on the top (from left to right) are the Presidential Unit Citation, the Navy Meritorious Unit Commendation with two bronze stars, and the China Service Medal. Other awards were for the various campaigns from 1943 to 1945. (Al Adcock)

The single main mast contains the SPS-10 Surface Search Radar on the fore mast extension and the SPN-43 Carrier Control Approach (CCA) on the aft extension. The SPN-35 Final Approach Radar antenna housing was removed in 1991. It occupied the aft island section area on the Navigation Bridge. (Al Adcock)

A cover was fitted over LEXINGTON's exhaust stack in Corpus Christi to prevent rain, weather, and birds from entering the exhaust ducts. The exhausts were angled during modernization to direct gases away from the radar antennas. Pri-Fly is located on the port side of the island, below the SPS-40 antenna. LEXINGTON's flight deck is used to display various US Navy aircraft, including a McDonnell F2H-2 Banshee with folded wings. (Al Adcock)

The SPS-40 Air Search Radar antenna is mounted on a platform at island deck level 011 on the port side. Above the SPS-40 antenna is the SPN-43 Carrier Control Approach radar antenna, located on a platform attached to the main mast. The URN-20 TACtical Air Navigation (TACAN) antenna sits atop the main mast. Various whip antennas are situated around the island for Ultra High Frequency (UHF), Very High Frequency (VHF), and Frequency Modulation (FM) radio sets. Additional whip antennas for these radios were installed along the flight deck. (Al Adcock)

A 40mm anti-aircraft gun crew watches while a fighter (out of the picture) recovers aboard LEXINGTON on 19 June 1944, after countering a Japanese air attack off Saipan. The number 3 and 4 twin 5 inch (12.7 cm)/38 caliber mounts are situated just below the 40mm mount. The 20mm gun galleries are located along the deck edge. (Real War Photos)

A 40mm Bofors quad-mount Mk 2 crew is in full mode action in 1944. Only the gun captain and a loader are not wearing army-type helmets introduced in 1942. Later helmets featured extended sides and backs for added protection and to provide room for headphones. Many spent shell casings litter the gun tub base. (US Navy)

Some of LEXINGTON's aircrew relax against the Number 4 twin 5 inch turret. Four of these turrets were mounted along the starboard side and were controlled by the Mk 37 gun director. The turret was faced with .75 inch (1.9 cm) steel, which protected the gun crew against only shrapnel and small caliber rounds. (US Navy via Frank Tanton)

Heavy Anti-Aircraft Weapons

5 inch (12.7 cm) Twin Gun Turret

5 inch Single Gun

LEXINGTON was fitted with four single mount 5 inch/38 caliber dual-purpose guns. These were all installed in port side gun sponsons – two guns forward and two weapons aft. These 5 inch guns were directed by the Mk 57 director. (US Navy via Frank Tanton)

Light Anti-Aircraft Weapons

40MM Quad Mount

20MM Twin Mount

20MM Single Mount

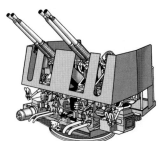

.50 Caliber (12.7MM) Quad Mount

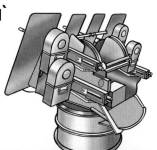

A 20MM gun crew relaxes between actions on LEXINGTON in 1945. The 20MM Oerlikon cannon was a Swiss design built under license in the United States and adapted for aircraft and naval use. The drum fed ammunition magazine held 60 rounds and the gun could fire up to 450 rounds per minute. One crewman wears the newly introduced flak helmet, which offered more protection than the Army style worn by the other crew. (US Navy)

LEXINGTON was fitted with seven Army type quad mounted .50 caliber (12.7MM) Browning M2 HB machine guns in the 20MM gun galleries during her March of 1945 refit. The Navy added this weapon to several carriers in response to the *kamikaze* threat. The .50 caliber weapons could put more rounds into the air than the 20MM cannon. (Al Adcock)

The 40mm Bofors quad mounted guns were the mainstay of the LEXINGTON's anti-aircraft armament. Thirteen quad mounts were installed along deck-side, the island, and the stern. Each mount had a crew of 11 men: the gun captain, one pointer, one trainer, four first loaders and four second loaders. The Bofors cannon was designed in Sweden and license built in the United States. (Al Adcock)

LEXINGTON has restored her two aft starboard 40mm quad mounts. A US ensign flies from a staff fitted to the flight deck ramp, or round down. The Douglas EKA-3B Skywarrior spotted on the aft flight deck operated as an electronic and tanker aircraft and was the largest aircraft to operate from LEXINGTON. (Al Adcock)

Two 40mm quad mounts along the starboard side have their gun barrels elevated. The barrels were water cooled and utilized springs to lessen their recoil. The 40mm guns had a range of 11,000 yards (10,058.4 m) and each gun had a firing rate of 160 rounds per minute. The gun crew's trainer stood to starboard of the weapon. (Al Adcock)

Cylindrical containers for modern life rafts and preservers are situated around one of LEXINGTON's starboard 40mm Mk 2 quad mounts. The containers protected the lifesaving equipment from the weather until used. All of LEXINGTON's 40mm guns were removed during her 1953-55 refit and the weapons installed on her today are representative guns for display purposes. (Al Adcock)

The port side forward 5 inch gun sponson now stands empty and unmanned. Two single mount weapons were fitted here during World War Two. Sand covering this deck was due to sandblasting occurring on LEXINGTON in an attempt to control rust and corrosion. (Al Adcock)

This practice loading machine allowed 40MM loaders and assistant loaders to improve their skills. It had the capability of cycling the rounds and elevating. The four-round clips had to be loaded quickly to maintain a rate of fire of 160 rounds per minute, or almost one clip per second. Spent shells were ejected to the rear of this machine, instead of the forward ejection on actual 40MM guns. (Al Adcock)

The American flag flies from its staff on LEXINGTON's island while its deck is prepared for yet another flight of SBDs and TBFs. Two SBD Dauntlesses are spotted at the aft end of the deck, while a TBF Avenger with its wings folded is located along the starboard side. The 5 inch gun crews relax atop the turrets awaiting the next action. (US Navy)

A Mk 12 Mod 4 radar antenna is mounted atop a Mk 37 Gun Director. The smaller antenna alongside the Mk 12 is for the Mk 22 Mod 0 radar. This gun director worked with the eight twin-mounted 5 inch guns on LEXINGTON's starboard side, while the radar antennas provided range and height information to the gun layers in the turrets. (Al Adcock)

The Mk 12 Mod 4 radar antenna was mounted on a metal frame atop the Mk 37 gun director. This radar could track the range, speed, and bearing of air and surface targets in all lighting and weather conditions. The Mk 22 height finding radar antenna mounted to the Mk 12's starboard side aided in tracking targets for the 5 inch gun crews. (Al Adcock)

LEXINGTON was fitted with the latest radar and electronic gear available at her 1943 commissioning. The large 'bed spring' on the main mast is the SK air search radar, which gave the carrier early warning of an impending air attack. Atop the main mast is the SG surface search radar. A 40mm quad mount is located above the navigation bridge. The Mk 37 gun director above the 40mm guns is topped by a Mk 12 radar antenna. (Floating Drydock)

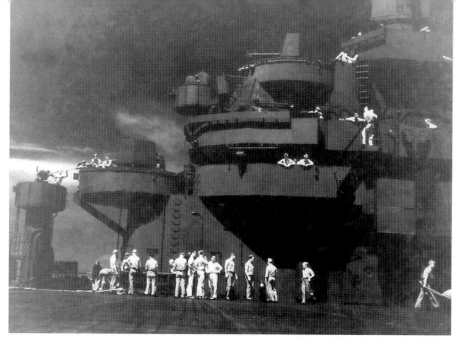

Officers and men take a few moments to relax before their next flight is assembled on LEXINGTON in November of 1943. The carrier was steaming under overcast skies towards the Gilbert and Marshall Islands for a raid on Japanese installations. An ordnance man dollies a 500-pound (226.8 KG) bomb to an aircraft spotted on the aft flight deck. (US Navy)

A SBD-5 Dauntless of VB-16 departs LEXINGTON to support the invasion of Saipan on 13 June 1944. The radio operator/rear gunner took the photograph from his seat soon after launch. LEXINGTON was equipped with two H-4 hydraulic catapults, but her starboard catapult was not used because of the ample wind coming across her deck. (Real War Photos)

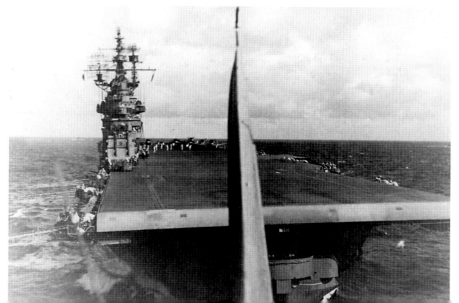

The port side of LEXINGTON's island serves as the scoreboard for Carrier Air Group Nineteen (CVG-19) in December of 1944. Japanese 'rising sun' ensigns signify the 450 aircraft CVG-19's aircraft shot down while flying off this carrier. The 370 painted on the lower island side indicated the number of feet from the bow and gave a visual clue to both the flight deck officers and aircrew. Bugs Bunny is painted on the upper island superstructure. (US Navy)

Aircrew and deck crew move toward a waiting aircraft on LEXINGTON's port side, while other crewmen congregate near the island. Red and yellow stripes mark the boundary of the forward Number One elevator. All deck crewmen wear a helmet containing ear and eye protection and – in some cases – earphones for radio communications. (Al Adcock)

A convex mirror is mounted to the navigation bridge area in 1976. This mirror allowed the Captain to have a panoramic view of the flight deck to his immediate rear. A group of visitors gather at LEXINGTON's bow, while her flight deck is clear of aircraft. The carrier was open for public tours while docked at NAS Pensacola, Florida. (Al Adcock)

'Vulture's row' was always occupied when flight operations were underway, since it afforded the best view of the deck. Pri-Fly occupied the upper level and the television crew occupied the lower level of LEXINGTON's port side island structure. Every landing is recorded and televised to the Captain and the ready rooms. (Al Adcock)

In 1976, the island's front was painted black in an effort to cover the jet exhaust staining. THINK! was a popular word in the 1970s and could be seen almost everywhere, including LEXINGTON. The entire island below the navigation deck level was painted black by 1988. (Al Adcock)

The message BEWARE OF PROPELLERS INTAKES & JET BLAST is painted on the aft port island. This warning is taken most seriously by all flight deck crewmen, since one small mistake could be their last. (Al Adcock)

LEXINGTON is berthed at Pensacola in 1977, with a gangway extended to the pier. The flight crew escalator is enclosed within the angled structure below the island. This escalator allowed flight crews to travel between the ready rooms and the flight deck. A navigation radar antenna is mounted on the forward Mk 37 gun director base on the island, while the aft Mk 37 base is left vacant. (Al Adcock)

The SG surface search radar antenna is mounted atop LEXINGTON's mainmast in early 1944. The large SK air search antenna is mounted to starboard of the funnel, with an SC-2 long range search antenna to port of the SK. A YE homing beacon is fitted atop the foremast extension, with the SG surface search antenna immediately below and forward of the YE. The SM fighter control radar antenna is located atop the foremast. (Floating Drydock)

The SG radar antenna is positioned atop of the main mast, with the IFF antennas positioned on the yardarms. An SC-2 long-range air search radar antenna is located aft of the main mast. Most sailors aboard LEXINGTON were oblivious to both the function of these antennas and the importance of electronic equipment to the war effort. (Floating Drydock)

LEXINGTON's funnel and masts supported her radar antenna array. Identification Friend or Foe (IFF) antennas were mounted on the yardarms high on the main mast, which is mounted on the funnel. IFF uses coded radio signals to interrogate aircraft, determining whether or not they are friendly. (Floating Drydock)

Anti-Aircraft Fire Control Directors

Mk 37 Director with Mk 12 Radar Antenna

Mk 37 Director with Mk 12 and Mk 22 Radar Antennas

Mk 37 Director with Mk 25 Radar Antenna

Mk 57 Director

A VF-16 F6F-3 launches from LEXINGTON in 1943, while crewmates watch from 'vulture's row.' The extensive radar antenna array is silhouetted against the sky and her Mk 37 fire control directors are positioned fore and aft on the island. The famous wartime photographer Commander Edward Steichen, USNR took this photograph while assigned to LEXINGTON. (US Navy)

A VT-4 T-2B Buckeye makes a touch-and-go on LEXINGTON in the early 1970s. An SPS-43 long-range air search radar is mounted on an extension fitted to the island's starboard side. Its antenna was the largest fitted to any US Navy ship. The Mk 25 radar equipped fire control system is still fitted, although the 5-inch guns were removed in the early 1960s. (Mike Slover)

LEXINGTON is displayed at Corpus Christi with the final radar antenna array she received prior to her decommissioning in 1991. An SPS-40 air search radar antenna is mounted on a platform fitted to her port upper island, while an SPN-43 antenna is mounted high on the mast and offset to port. Various naval aircraft and tourists cover the flight deck. (Al Adcock)

Catapult operations are viewed from the forward section of the Primary Flight Control (Pri-Fly) area and are reported aft to the Air-Boss. This position has a view of the forward deck and catapult, along with the two elevators. All of the wiring running along the overhead is for the extensive communications and command and control devices. (Al Adcock)

Pri-Fly has the responsibility of all air operations on the deck. The Air-Boss and his deputy the Mini-Boss control all flight deck activity from the catapult to the Landing Signal Officer (LSO). The Air-Boss occupies the port seat and the Mini-Boss the starboard seat. (Al Adcock)

The Pri-Fly area has the best view of the deck area, which was being prepared for flight operations in 1988. LEXINGTON's portside Number Two catapult was deactivated leaving the Number One catapult to handle all launches. Signal flags ran down from the mainmast yardarms in front of the Pri-Fly windows. (Al Adcock)

The arresting cable pressure settings are entered into the unit behind the Air-Boss' seat. The settings are determined by the landing aircraft's gross weight. If the setting is too light, the aircraft would go too far down the landing area once engaging the landing wire. Too heavy a pressure setting could rip the tail hook off the aircraft. (Al Adcock)

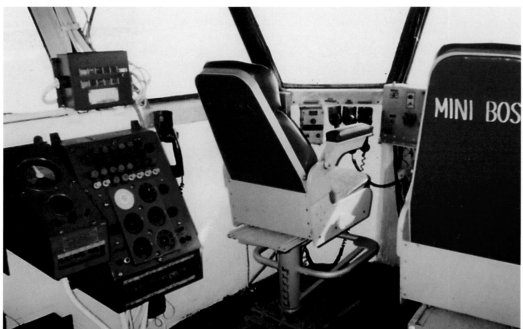

Hydraulic pressure settings for LEXINGTON's four arresting cables are set in this device, located in Pri-Fly. The large ramp clearance gauge is located on the port side of the device, with the aircraft hook/eye distance in feet gauge below this. Gauge setting operators in Pri-Fly are in radio contact with the landing aircraft to determine the amount of fuel aboard, which determines the aircraft's landing weight. (Al Adcock)

41

The foam cannon is located on the signal flag platform, where flag signals are sent. This cannon can spray smothering foam, which denies oxygen to the fire. Foam for the cannon is sent from storage tanks below decks through a pipe running along the island's port side. The hull number 16 directly above the foam cannon position is white with black shadowing. (Al Adcock)

The foam cannon is the only cannon on LEXINGTON that could put out a fire; the other cannons started fires. A crewman grasped the tubular handle to aim the cannon at any fires in his vicinity. The port side elevator's outline lacks the red and yellow dashed outline of the Number One elevator on the forward flight deck. (Al Adcock)

A foam cannon for fighting deck fires is located on the port side of LEXINGTON's island, in the flag signal position. The crewman standing by the cannon wears ear protectors against the loud noise of aircraft engines on the flight deck. A-6E Intruders line up in 'the street' area prior to launching from the Number One catapult. A C-1A Trader is parked with its wings folded on the bow. (Al Adcock)

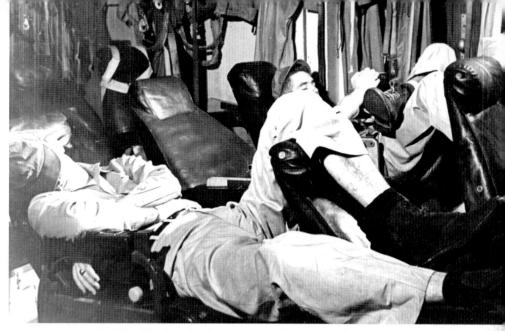

Pilots relax in one of LEXINGTON's ready rooms between flight operations against Tarawa on 17 September 1943. The pilots sitting here are (left to right): Lt (Jg) W. C. Birkholm, Lt (Jg) C.L. Nunn, Lt (Jg) W.W. Reiter, Ens A.R. Fizalkowski, Lt (Jg) C.H. Blome, and Ens A. Durham. (Real War Photos)

An Air Intelligence Officer (AIO) questions two pilots of Carrier Air Group Twenty (CVG-20) after a raid on the Formosa Strait in January of 1945. The pilots were asked about air defenses, the number and type of aircraft encountered, and perceived results of the raid. The middle pilot wears a China-Burma-India (CBI) Theatre of Operations patch on his left sleeve. (Real War Photos)

When pilots are not flying, they love to sleep. These pilots are snoozing between raids on Formosa (now Taiwan) in 1945. Their flight boots are not laced all the way up in case they must take them off in the event of a water landing. The leather covered ready room seat was the most comfortable seat available at the time. (Real War Photos)

Pilots from Torpedo Squadron Twenty (VT-20) discuss the raid on the Formosa Strait in January of 1945. The pilots are (from left): Lt (Jg) R D Olson, Ens John J McIntosh, and Lt (Jg) W C Pohtilla. The average age of the pilots in LEXINGTON's Air Groups was 24 years old. (Real War Photos)

43

Pilots listen attentively as the AIO gives them a preflight briefing. One pilot in the second row is wearing a Mae West life preserver marked VS-27 (for Scouting Squadron Twenty Seven) and he is not wearing any socks. This turnout may be due to his having been in the 'drink' (the ocean) once before. (US Navy)

Enlisted aircrew – radio operator/gunners on dive-bombers and torpedo bombers – await the pilots and the call to man aircraft during World War Two. They are wearing yellow Mae West personal floating devices and parachute harnesses. While officers wore khaki uniforms for flight duties, enlisted aircrew wore light blue shirts and dark blue trousers. All Navy flight crews wore canvas helmets with integral earphones and goggles. (US Navy)

The sight every returning pilots waits for – his Landing Signal Officer (LSO) on his carrier. Lt (Jg) 'Bud' Deering is the LSO bringing aboard an aircraft following a raid in the Marshall and Gilbert Chain of Islands in November of 1943. Lt Butler is the assistant LSO standing behind Lt Deering and is ready to take over if needed. (US Navy)

LCdr Paul D. Buie (center), commander of VF-16, briefs his pilots aboard LEXINGTON during the Gilberts Operation in late 1943. They crouch beside one of the Squadron's F6F-3 Hellcat fighters. Buie and two other pilots have a red stripe on their canvas helmets; however, its significance is unknown. Today's naval aviators wear dark green flight suits and hard plastic helmets. (US Navy)

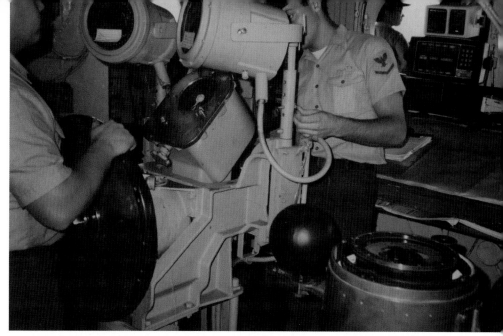

The helmsman (left) and the engine order telegraph operator man the con aboard LEXINGTON. Their watch position is in the armored pilothouse immediately aft of the Navigation Bridge. The helmsman receives his steering orders from the Officer of the Deck. These crewmen wear black ball caps with the ship's name (USS LEXINGTON) and pennant number (AVT-16) in gold. (Al Adcock)

The armored pilothouse is silent in 1999, while LEXINGTON is moored at Corpus Christi. Key items are (from left): the engine room telegraph, the helm with repeating compass, and the ship's magnetic binnacle compass. The Navigation Bridge is viewed through the ports and portals. (Al Adcock)

The helmsman stands at the helm, with a rudder angle indicator above and forward of it. Two repeater gyrocompasses are mounted above the rudder angle indicator. These devices aid the helmsman in guiding the ship. The ship's magnetic compass binnacle is to starboard of the helm and is flanked by two black iron balls, which compensate for the ship's own magnetic field. (Al Adcock)

The navigator's station and chart table was located on deck Level 6. It is separated from the pilothouse by the captain's cabin. The navigator plotted the course of the ship on the table adjacent to the bulkhead. Drawers within the table held charts, pens, and other tools for the navigator's use. (Al Adcock)

Ordnance crews chalk 'love letters' to the Japanese on 1000 pound (453.6 KG) bombs before the 18-19 September 1943 raid on Tarawa. The message included "To Tojo, from the boys of the W.O." and "Here's one for you Tojo." The Ordnance Department (V-5) was responsible for all bombs, torpedoes, guns, and rockets that were hung on the embarked Air Group's aircraft. (US Navy)

Pilots walk past an F6F-3 Hellcat (38) while heading for their aircraft aboard LEXINGTON in the summer of 1943. The national insignia on the Hellcat's fuselage has a red border, which was authorized on US aircraft from 28 June 1943. It was officially replaced with a blue border on 31 July 1943, although the red trim persisted for several months. (Real War Photos)

Torpedo bomber pilots gather in VT-16's ready room aboard LEXINGTON on 17 September 1943. The blackboard contains aircraft assignments and landing and takeoff details for the crews. The pilots are (from left): LCdr R H Isley, Ens H Dana, Lt (Jg) E F Teruasky, and Lt N A Sterrie. They and their colleagues flew TBF Avengers in raids on Tarawa in September. (Real War Photos)

Ordnance men roll 500 pound (226.8 KG) bombs on LEXINGTON's hangar deck prior to a raid on Okinawa in February of 1945. Raised bands on the bombs increased their shrapnel effect upon detonation. The bombs were raised from the bomb storage rooms to the hangar deck on ordnance elevators. Tailfins and fuses were added when the bombs were loaded on the aircraft. (US Navy)

Cots covered LEXINGTON's hangar deck for in-transit naval personnel and their gear in the Eastern Pacific. Her hangar deck covered approximately 40,000 square feet (3716 M2) of area. Since there was no assigned Air Group, the hangar deck was turned into a huge barracks ship. Curtains used to separate the three hangar bay sections are folded along the sides. (Real War Photos)

An ordnance man carries a 5-inch (12.7 CM) High Velocity Aerial Rocket (HVAR) past a VT-16 TBF-1C Avenger. The HVAR was used against ships and static enemy targets. The rocket's 5-inch warhead was fitted to a 3.5-inch (8.9 CM) rocket motor and gave the Avenger the firepower of a destroyer. TBF-1Cs were equipped to carry eight HVARs under its wings. (US Navy)

Ordnance men aboard LEXINGTON prepare to load M-69 incendiary clusters into the bomb bays of awaiting Eastern Aircraft TBM-1 Avengers. The aircraft were being readied for Operation TASK FORCE, a raid on Hollandia, New Guinea on 8 May 1944. The incendiary weapons were designed to cause fires in Japanese wooden emplacements, housing, and barracks. (US Navy)

One of the ready rooms aboard LEXINGTON has been reconfigured to its World War Two era configuration. The leather recliners were comfortable compared to the aircraft seat the pilots occupied when manning their aircraft. Small desks immediately in front of the chairs gave pilots a firm surface to write notes during the briefings. Each squadron aboard the carrier had its own ready room. (Al Adcock)

The Flag Bridge interior is called the Flag Plot and would have been occupied by an Admiral and his associated staff while LEXINGTON was at sea. The Flag Bridge was located on Deck Level 5, one deck below the Navigation Bridge. The Flag Bridge was armored like the Navigation Bridge and was also fitted with armored view ports. (Al Adcock)

The Flag Bridge was fitted with armored, one inch (2.5 CM) thick view ports, which could be raised to protect the 'Flag' area's occupants from projectiles and shrapnel. The view ports were increased from two to three during LEXINGTON's 1962 refit. She assumed the training carrier role after this refit. (Al Adcock)

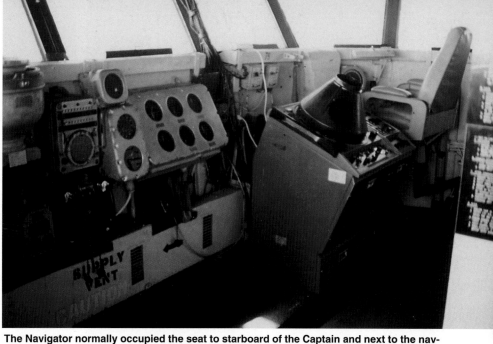

LEXINGTON's Captain occupied the 'Big Chair' on the port side of the Navigation Bridge. This bridge was enclosed during the 1953-55 refit and glass was added to the roof. Heat from the sun resulted in the roof glass being painted blue. Sound deadening material was later installed over the tinted windows. (Al Adcock)

The Navigator normally occupied the seat to starboard of the Captain and next to the navigation radar. The scope of this radar had a conical hood to allow reading the scope under all light conditions. The cluster of six instruments on the forward bulkhead indicated the ship's course, speed, wind direction, and engine settings. (Al Adcock)

The Captain's chair is located in the port forward corner of the Navigation Bridge, across from the Navigator's chair. Various navigation and engine instruments are located along the forward bulkhead. Sound deadening material covering the bulkheads and roof area dampens the jet engine noise, which can reach up to 150 decibels. (Al Adcock)

Although the Captain's day quarters were not stately, the crews' berthing was entirely spartan. The crew berthing areas were placed throughout the ship on most decks and were usually close to their duty stations. These berths are in the area of frame number 184 on the second deck below the hangar deck. (Al Adcock)

The crew head on deck level two was just off of the crew berthing area immediately below the hangar deck. The head consisted of toilet facilities and stainless steel lavatories. When women were welcomed aboard LEXINGTON from the early 1980s, separate facilities were configured for the female sailors and officers. (Al Adcock)

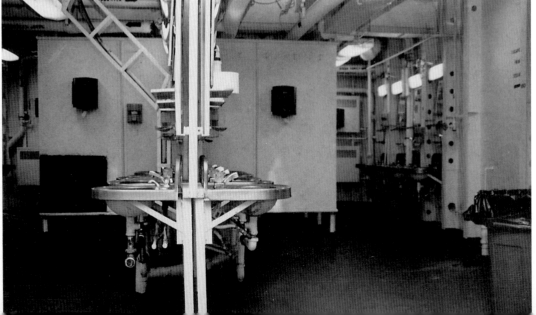

The Captain's day cabin is located just off of the Navigation Bridge on the port side of Deck Level 6. His cabin is paneled in walnut and contains a bed, a simple pull-up chair, and a table. The head (bathroom) is adjacent to the chair. This cabin is located close to the bridge, allowing the Captain to be close at hand to handle his duties. (Al Adcock)

Another view of crew berthing reveals the small space available for personal items. Life at sea was not like being on a cruise ship and required a certain mind-set. This included the requirement of spartan living conditions with the full knowledge that shore leave would soon be a reality. (Al Adcock)

LEXINGTON's sick bay area is centrally located on deck level 2, below the hangar deck to handle any emergency that might arise. The hospital bay contained beds that could be raised to make room for stretcher patients. Two doctors and 14 corpsman took care of the crew's medical needs. (Al Adcock)

LEXINGTON's Compliment

1943	275 Officers, 2365 Enlisted (Including Air Group)	
1955	335 Officers, 3185 Enlisted (Including Air Group)	
1988	75 Officers, 1368 Enlisted (No Air Group Embarked)	

A caricature of LEXINGTON is painted on the wall of the ship's barbershop. It depicts the launching and recovery of aircraft in a whimsical manner. The artwork was completed by crewmembers following the lead of artist Frank Caruso. LEXINGTON and other aircraft carriers have many of the services and amenities of a small town for its large crew. These include a barber shop, ship's store, snack bar, library, hospital, and newspaper. (Al Adcock)

51

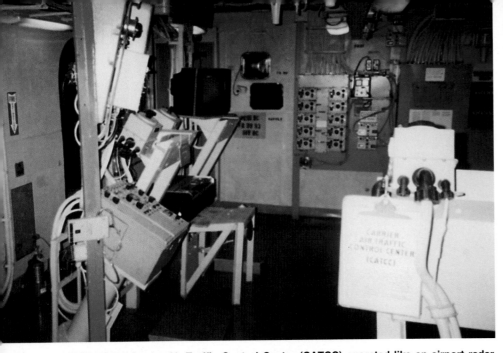

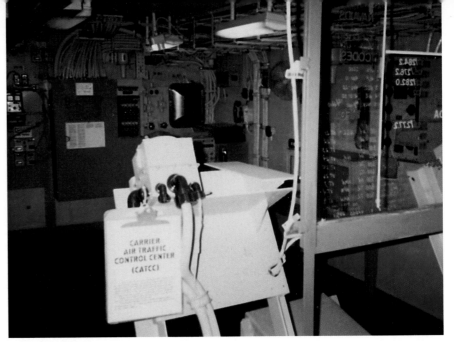

LEXINGTON's Carrier Air Traffic Control Center (CATCC) operated like an airport radar approach facility. The CATCC – located amidships on the gallery deck – coordinated flights with the Federal Aviation Administration (FAA) during flight operations in the Gulf of Mexico. Four radar operators vectored the incoming aircraft on approach to the carrier. (Al Adcock)

The Air Operations (AirOps) status board in the CATCC keeps the flight director posted on all incoming and departing aircraft. This information is coordinated with both the Combat Information Center (CIC) located near the CATCC and the FAA ashore. The personnel responsible with keeping the status current had to write it backward on the board. (Al Adcock)

The CATCC's duty deck faces the AirOps status board. Its duty officer is responsible for all air traffic in LEXINGTON's vicinity and for the coordination with the CIC. The red telephone in the center is a secure phone for intership communications. This would be used to communicate sensitive information to the captain and task force commander. Other telephones on the desk were used for non-secure transmission with other parts of the ship. (Al Adcock)

This windlass capstan on the fantail was used to bring in ropes for docking. One end of the rope is wrapped around the capstan, while the other end is secured to the dock. The portal aft of the windlass leads to the hangar bay. A black non-slip paint covers this section of the hangar deck. (Al Adcock)

A sectioned radial engine and other exhibits are displayed in LEXINGTON's center hangar area in 1999. She had three hangar areas, which were separated by blast doors and black-out curtains. The doors were closed in the event of an air attack, while the curtains were drawn to allow work in an area open to the sea. (Al Adcock)

A docking rope is wrapped on a reel secured to the port side of LEXINGTON's fantail. The rope is played out from this reel, around the nearby windlass capstan, and out to the dock. Docking ropes are currently made from synthetic materials, which are stronger and more durable than the natural fibers used when LEXINGTON first entered service in 1943. (Al Adcock)

53

LEXINGTON's hurricane bow contains the 'bull nose' down below the catapult overruns, called 'horns.' These are designed to catch the catapult launch bridles. Safety netting is installed along the flight deck edge. The devices hanging from the overruns are lights used to illuminate the ship at night. Her bow was enclosed during the 1953-55 refit to prevent water from washing into the forecastle and below decks. (Al Adcock)

The port catapult overrun was designed to give slightly increased deck room for the launched aircraft. Port and starboard overruns were added during a refit to configure the deck as the larger fleet carriers. The safety netting provided some safety to the bridle runners and other flight deck personnel when in that deck area. (Al Adcock)

LEXINGTON retains her starboard anchor while berthed at Corpus Christi, while the port anchor is displayed at the Museum's entrance. Each anchor weighed approximately 30,000 pounds (13,608 KG) and was controlled by the forward windlass room in the forecastle. (Al Adcock)

The carrier's port anchor is displayed at the entrance to the USS LEXINGTON Museum in Corpus Christi. It was forged at Norfolk Navy Yard, Virginia in 1940 and installed on LEXINGTON in 1943. The anchor is displayed with several links of anchor chain. Each chain link weighs 130 pounds (59 KG). (Al Adcock)

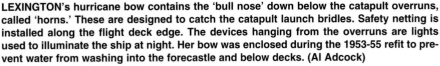

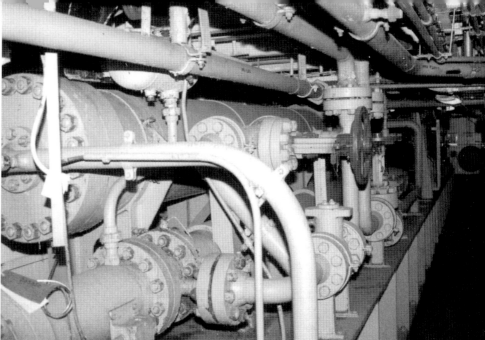

(Above) Two anchor chain windlasses are fitted in LEXINGTON's windlass room, which is located in her forecastle (foc'sle). Each anchor chain runs from the windlass to the anchor, located on each side of her bow. Windlass brake stations are fitted to the deck along the chains' route. Anchor chain lengths ranged from 810 feet (246.9 м) to 1080 feet (329.2 м) in length. (Al Adcock)

(Above Right) The starboard catapult return engine is located near the aft end of LEXINGTON's catapult on the hangar deck level. Another such engine is located on the port side. Steam pressure from the boiler rooms drove the piston inside the cylinder. Each of LEXINGTON's two C-11 catapults could launch a 60,000 pound (27,216 KG) aircraft with a maximum end speed of 130 knots (149.7 MPH/240.9 KMH). (Al Adcock)

(Right) A throttle man checks his gauges in one of LEXINGTON's four boiler control rooms. The gauges indicated steam pressures and temperatures in various steam lines, which sent steam to either the turbo generators or the catapults. The eight Babcock & Wilcox boilers produced steam for four geared Westinghouse turbines, which combined to produce 150,000 horsepower. This power enabled LEXINGTON to maintain a speed of 33 knots (38 MPH/61.2 KMH). (US Navy)

A hook runner races out to disengage the arresting hook on a landing Douglas SBD-5 Dauntless. The SBD had just returned to LEXINGTON from a raid on the Marshall and Gilbert islands in November of 1943. The deck arresting cables were raised off the wooded flight deck by 'fiddle bars.' These bars each resembled the bridge that raises the strings over a fiddle's body. The 'fiddle bars' lowered the cables to allow aircraft to taxi forward after the hook runner has disengaged the arresting hook. These bars were then raised for the next aircraft to recover aboard the ship. (US Navy)

LEXINGTON's flight deck was originally built of Douglas fir over a steel decking. When the deck was angled in 1953-55, various types of construction were incorporated. Plywood and pressure treated hard woods were employed with a coating of non-slip paint. The deck is presently undergoing a restoration, which will cost many hundred of thousands of dollars. (Al Adcock)

A civilian construction crew repairs the landing area of LEXINGTON's flight deck in 1976. Fir planks are laid out prior to their installation on the deck. The planking was covered with black non-skid paint to seal the finish against the elements. Current US aircraft carriers employ a steel flight deck to take the heavier weights of today's aircraft. (Al Adcock)

LEXINGTON's crew 'man the rails' while the ship steams into Pensacola Harbor in 1989. A T-28 Trojan is spotted by the port catapult, while the A-4 Skyhawk parked aft is painted in the colors of the US Navy's Blue Angels Air Demonstration Squadron, which is based at NAS Pensacola. LEXINGTON's flight deck modifications – including installation of the angled flight deck and deck edge elevators – increased her later dimensions over her orig-inal specifications. Her overall length increased from 872 feet (265.8 M) as built in 1943 to 910 feet (277.4 M) at decommissioning in 1991, while her overall beam went from 147 feet 6 inches (45 M) to 166 feet 10 inches (50.9 M). Three tugs along the carrier's port side help guide the carrier towards her berth. (Earl Caudell)

The forward Number One deck centerline elevator is lowered while LEXINGTON departs Puget Sound Naval Yard after her 1945 refit. Her paint scheme was changed from the earlier Measure 21 Navy Blue System to the Measure 12 Graded System. Measure 12 consisted of Sea Blue (5-S) on the lower hull and Ocean Gray (5-O) on the upper hull and superstructure. LEXINGTON's flight deck had three arresting cables forward and 11 on the aft deck, but the forward cables were rarely used. (Real War Photos)

(Above) Aircraft handlers move an F6F-5 Hellcat (3) from VF-20 onto LEXINGTON's port side Number Two elevator in December of 1944. The fighter was moved from the hangar deck to the flight deck prior to flight operations. US Navy fighters were painted overall Glossy Sea Blue (FS15042) from 13 March 1944. This scheme was authorized for all carrier-based aircraft from 7 October 1944. (US Navy)

(Left) LEXINGTON (CVA-16) steams in 1955, following her two year refit. This refit included the addition of two H-11 steam catapults and an angled flight deck with six arresting cables ('wires'). The flight deck was Dark Gray (FS36076), with white markings and a black metal reinforcement plate on the landing area. The four single 5 inch (12.7 CM) guns were retained and are supplemented by a pair of twin 3 inch (7.6 CM)/50 mounts and two single 5 inch mounts in the former forward starboard 20MM gun galleries. The starboard side deck-edge elevator is lowered to the hangar deck level. (Elsilrac)

Girder-type construction was used on the undersurface of the Number Two deck edge elevator. This elevator was used from LEXINGTON's commissioning in 1943 until it was deactivated and locked in the up position in the 1970s. The Number Two elevator became part of the flight deck when it was angled in the 1950s and its functioning would have interfered with flight operations. (Al Adcock)

The Number Three starboard side deck edge elevator is still operational and is used daily to move cargo and vehicles from the flight to the hangar deck and the concrete causeway leading to the beach. The Japanese flag on the island is the approximate area where the Japanese kamikaze suicide aircraft hit LEXINGTON on 5 November1944. (Al Adcock)

LEXINGTON (CVA-16) performs an underway replenishment in the Pacific in 1961. Her Number One elevator was modified in both shape and size in 1957. This allowed LEXINGTON to accommodate larger aircraft, including the North American AJ-2 Savage, the Douglas A3D-2 (later A-3B) Skywarrior, and the Grumman WF-2 (later E-1B) Tracker. The carrier embarked Carrier Air Group Twenty One (CVG-21) during this cruise, whose aircraft included FJ Furies along the starboard forward flight deck. A McDonnell F3H Demon and three Vought F8U (later F-8) Crusaders are parked ahead of the two catapults, while a WF-2 is spotted beside the island. The replenishment ship ALUBRA (AF-55) steams between LEXINGTON and the destroyer PARSONS (DD-949). LEXINGTON was reassigned as an anti-submarine carrier and redesignated CVS-16 on 1 October 1962. (Elsilrac)

(Above) LEXINGTON sails in the Gulf of Mexico in 1977, with a Kaman H-2 Seasprite utility helicopter spotted on her aft flight deck. LEXINGTON replaced ANTIETAM (CV-36) as the US Navy's only training carrier on 20 December 1962. She served in this role until decomissioned on 26 November 1991. LEXINGTON was responsible for the Carrier Qualifications ('Car Quals') of all Naval Aviators and Naval Flight Officers (NFOs) during that period. She also trained deck crews and future flight deck officers and LSOs. Her designation changed from CVS-16 to CVT-16 on 1 July 1969. (Via Mike Slover)

(Left) LEXINGTON (AVT-16) prepares for flight operations in the Gulf of Mexico in 1988. She was redesignated AVT-16 in July of 1978, reflecting her role as a fleet auxiliary. Flight deck crews sweep her deck for 'FOD' (Foreign Object Damage) prior to flight operations. 'FOD' – including nuts, bolts, and tools – could damage jet engines and cause failures. The hull number 16 on her flight deck bow was changed from solid white to a white outline during the 1980s. Several yellow-painted aircraft tugs and a white-and-red fire truck are parked near the island. (Art Giberson)

LEXINGTON is moored at pier side by Lexington Plaza, NAS Pensacola, Florida awaiting her fate in 1990. A pair of temporary equipment shelters are placed on her flight deck, opposite the island. Various committees in cities from Pensacola to Corpus Christi, Texas lobbied the US Navy to have LEXINGTON make their city her final port. (Via Mike Slover)

USS LEXINGTON Service Milestones

Commissioned (CV-16): 17 February 1943
Decommissioned: 23 April 1947
Redesignated CVA-16: 1 October 1952
  (While Ship was in Reserve)
Modernization Begun: 1 September 1953
Recommissioned: 15 August 1956
Redesignated CVS-16: 1 October 1962
Redesignated CVT-16: 16 January 1969
Redesignated AVT-16: 1 July 1978
Decommissioned: 26 November 1991

LEXINGTON is readied for her tow from Pensacola to Corpus Christi in 1991. The device on the forward flight deck was used to attach the tow cable to the anchor chain. Both catapult tracks were covered and she has received a fresh coat of paint for her presentation to the City of Corpus Christi. This included the hull and most of her superstructure in Haze Gray (5-H), with the forward island and masts in black. The flight deck is coated with black anti-skid paint, while deck markings are white and yellow. (Mike Slover)

61

LEXINGTON's ordnance men load a 2000 pound (907.2 KG) Bliss-Leavitt Mk 13 torpedo into the bomb bay of a VT-16 TBF-1 Avenger in September of 1943. The Avenger was a dual-purpose bomber, able to carry either 2000 pounds of bombs or one torpedo. TBF/TBM Avengers were embarked on LEXINGTON from 1943 until its decommissioning in 1946. (US Navy)

The Air Department's V-2 deck crew keeps in shape with some calisthenics on LEXINGTON's flight deck in November of 1943. The deck is covered with aircraft from Carrier Air Group Sixteen (CVG-16), which are being readied for a raid on Tarawa. F6F Hellcats are spotted behind the exercising crew, followed by TBF Avengers and SBD Dauntlesses. (US Navy)

Vice Admiral Marc A. Mitscher, Commander of Task Force 58, sits on LEXINGTON's Flag Bridge on 19 June 1944. Admiral Mitscher endeared himself to all Naval Aviators during the Battle of the Philippine Sea that month, when he ordered all deck lights and carrier searchlights turned on to guide the returning aircraft. This risky action – exposing the carriers to potential Japanese submarine attack – saved many US aircraft and aviators. (US Navy)

LEXINGTON stands out of Alameda, California on 29 May 1945. She has a deck load of aircraft for the Pacific Theater and the last push toward Japan. Her aft flight deck is covered with North American PBJs, the Navy/Marine patrol bomber version of the B-25 Mitchell. This brings back memories of the Doolittle Raid just three years earlier! (US Navy)

Admiral Mitscher congratulates Commander David McCampbell on his aerial victories over the Japanese on 29 October 1944. Mitscher was Commander of Task Force 58 with his flag on LEXINGTON. Commander McCampbell was Commander Air Group (CAG) 15 aboard ESSEX (CV-9). He scored 34 confirmed victories – the most for any US Naval Aviator – by the end of World War Two. (US Navy)

LEXINGTON rests today at her permanent mooring at Corpus Christi, Texas. A concrete causeway leads from the beach to the ship. Visitors board the carrier over the lowered starboard deck edge elevator. The flight deck has a representative display of various US Navy aircraft arranged along her flight deck. These include an EKA-3B Skywarrior at the stern and a McDonnell F-4A Phantom II on the bow. The Texas State Aquarium is located onshore, near the LEXINGTON Museum. (Carol Adcock)

The 'Blue Ghost' is all lit up for nighttime viewing by visitors to Corpus Christi. LEXING-TON earned her nickname after Japanese radio propaganda announcer 'Tokyo Rose' proclaimed her sunk four times during World War Two. Her reports of LEXINGTON's sinking were greatly exaggerated, since the 'Fighting Lady' can still be viewed today. LEXINGTON had lights for use while in port during her Navy service, although they were not as extensive as the ones she uses today in Corpus Christi. (Carol Adcock)

LEXINGTON lies at anchor at Puget Sound Navy Yard in Bremerton, Washington on 16 February 1944. She had just completed a refit, which included repairs following the Japanese torpedo attack off Kwajalein on 4 December 1943. LEXINGTON sailed back to the central Pacific after this refit to join the Fifth Fleet. The carrier returned to action when the Fifth Fleet attacked Mille Atoll in the Marshall Islands on 18 March 1944. She is camouflaged in Measure 21, the Navy Blue System. LEXINGTON's lattice radio antenna masts are raised along the sides of her flight deck. (Floating Drydock)

Following her refit in March of 1945, LEXINGTON was painted in Measure 12, the modified Graded System. The colors consisted of Ocean Gray (5-O) on the upper hull and superstructure and Sea Blue (5-S) on the lower hull. The deck was stained Deck Blue (20-B), with the hull number 16 in black on both the bow and stern. The armament was augmented by five Army type quad .50 caliber (12.7MM) machine guns in the 20MM gun galleries. (Floating Drydock)

LEXINGTON (CVA-16) arrives in San Francisco Bay, California in early 1958. She had just completed a four and one-half month long overhaul at Puget Sound Naval Shipyard. Crewmen spell out USO (for United Services Organization) on her forward deck to publicize a USO fundraising drive. The organization provides entertainment and social services to US armed forces personnel. The automobiles parked on the aft deck presumably belonged to crewmembers. (US Navy)

The catapult crew prepares to launch two North American FJ-4B Furies off LEXINGTON in June of 1959. The 'hurricane' style bow and catapult run offs were added during her 1956 refit at Puget Sound Navy Yard. Light standards were added to the port and starboard bow quarters at the same time. She still carries her 5 inch guns in the port sponsons, but the weapons were removed in the early 1960s. Grumman F11F Tiger fighters are spotted along the port edge of the flight deck. LEXINGTON is now painted in Measure 27, the current standard scheme for US Navy ships. This scheme had the hull and superstructure in Haze Gray (5-H). (Elsilrac)

LEXINGTON (CVS-16) steams in the Gulf of Mexico on 15 July 1963 – nearly seven months after assuming her training carrier duties. Midshipmen from the US Naval Academy in Annapolis, Maryland were aboard to observe carrier qualifications. LEXINGTON has 26 North American T-28C Trojan trainers spotted on her forward and center flight deck areas. The T-28 was originally developed for the US Air Force, but also served as the US Navy's basic trainer from 1953 until 1984. (US Navy)

LEXINGTON executes a turn to starboard while preparing to conduct 'car quals' (carrier qualifications) in the Gulf of Mexico in 1979. She was designated the US Navy's training carrier in 1962 and assigned to NAS Pensacola, Florida. Her flight deck is painted black with white markings. Several support vehicles are parked beside LEXINGTON's island. She did not embark any squadrons while serving in the training carrier role. All aircraft operating from LEXINGTON came from shore bases. (US Navy)

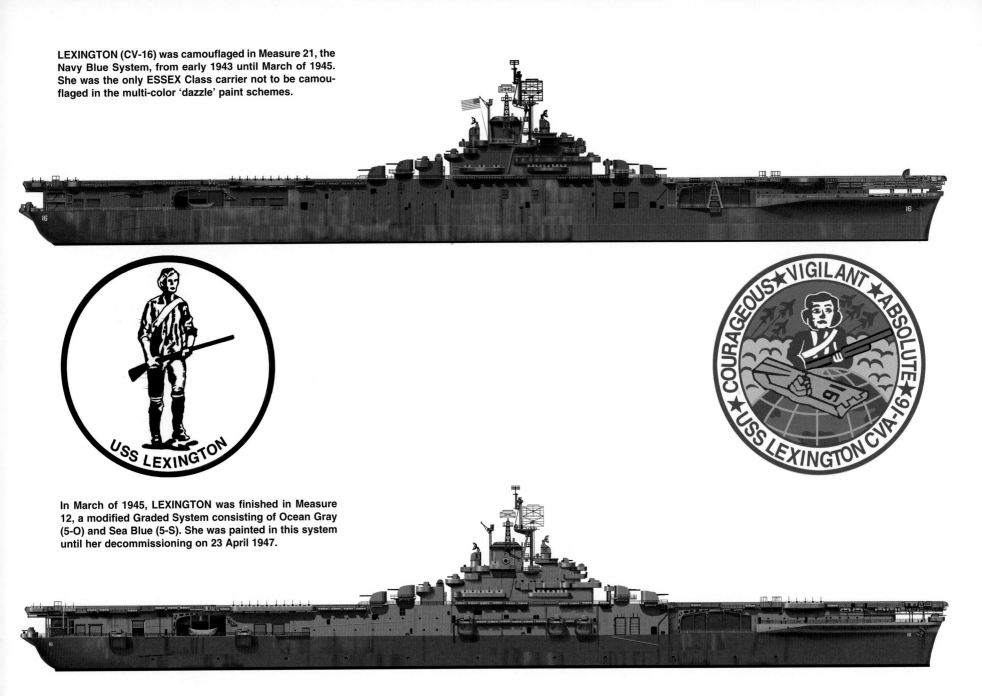

LEXINGTON (CV-16) was camouflaged in Measure 21, the
Navy Blue System, from early 1943 until March of 1945.
She was the only ESSEX Class carrier not to be camou-
flaged in the multi-color 'dazzle' paint schemes.

In March of 1945, LEXINGTON was finished in Measure
12, a modified Graded System consisting of Ocean Gray
(5-O) and Sea Blue (5-S). She was painted in this system
until her decommissioning on 23 April 1947.

USS LEXINGTON

COURAGEOUS ★ VIGILANT ★ ABSOLUTE ★
USS LEXINGTON CVA-16

LEXINGTON was refitted and modernized from 1953 to 1955 and was finished in Measure 27, the Haze Gray (5-H) scheme. She is armed with four 5 inch (12.7 CM)/38 caliber guns and four 3 inch (7.6 CM) guns.

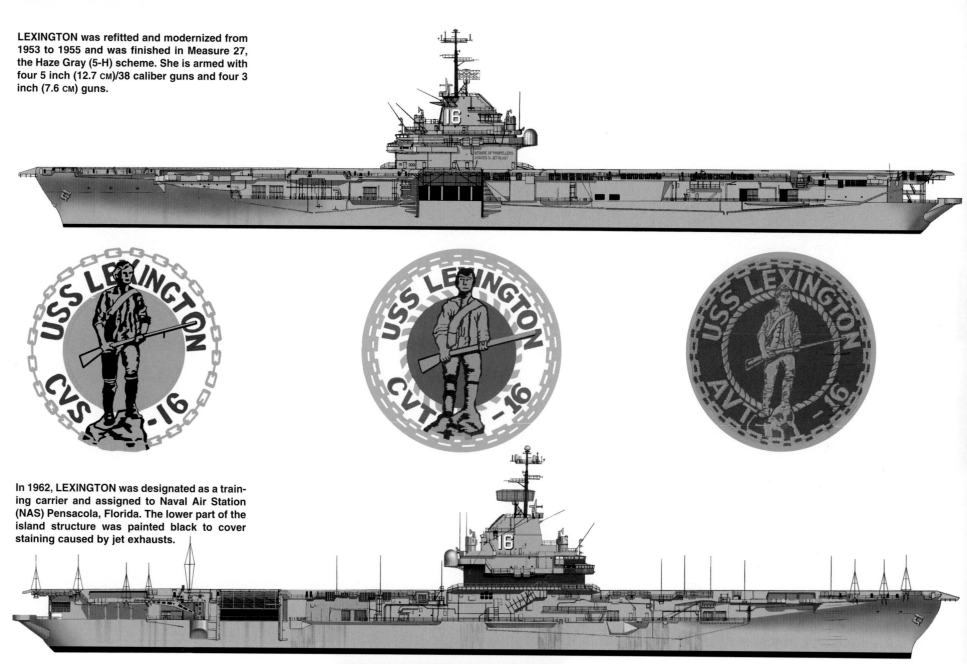

In 1962, LEXINGTON was designated as a training carrier and assigned to Naval Air Station (NAS) Pensacola, Florida. The lower part of the island structure was painted black to cover staining caused by jet exhausts.

Emblem on lower front of LEXINGTON's island during her training carrier period.

Sailors 'man the rails' while LEXINGTON is maneuvered to a pier at Pensacola in preparation for her decommissioning on 26 November 1991. A tug assisted the carrier to the pier, while pleasure boaters cruise near the warship. In a solemn ceremony, LEXINGTON was relieved from duty as a commissioned ship in the US Navy. She was returned to Pensacola NAS following the ceremony to await her fate. (US Navy)

Four tugs begin the process of moving LEXINGTON from the Pensacola City pier back to Sand Point, NAS Pensacola in 1991. After decommissioning the ship, the Navy removed equipment that was considered sensitive and still required some form of security clearance. The gas stack was covered to prevent entry of unwanted items, including birds and weather. (Art Giberson)

Tugs maneuver LEXINGTON through Pensacola Bay in 1991. She was under tow from the city pier back to NAS Pensacola for final disposal of sensitive equipment and to await her fate. Pensacola and Corpus Christi vied for the 'Blue Ghost,' with the Texas Gulf Coast city emerging victorious. (Art Giberson)

LEXINGTON returns to NAS Pensacola for the final time in December of 1991. Once all sensitive equipment was removed, the Navy turned her over to the Corpus Christi Area Convention and Visitors Bureau (CCACVB). The tow to Corpus Christi began on 24 January 1992. (US Navy)

LEXINGTON is under tow for the journey to Corpus Christi in late 1991. The port anchor is deployed in the ready to drop status if needed. The aircraft recovery crane is chained to the starboard deck-side in the area called the 'junk yard.' The tow from Pensacola to Corpus Christi took six days. (Art Giberson)

This Grumman F6F-3 Hellcat (13) was assigned to Fighting Squadron Sixteen (VF-16) aboard LEXINGTON in August of 1943. The US national insignia briefly included a red border, which was soon replaced by a blue surround.

The Douglas SBD-5 Dauntless (32) flew in both the scout and dive-bomber roles while serving with Bombing Squadron Sixteen (VB-16). This Squadron flew the SBD off LEXINGTON from May of 1943 until June of 1944.

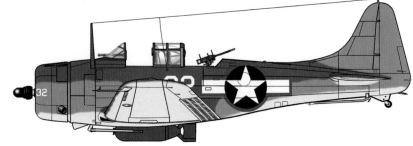

White 75 was a Curtiss SB2C-3 Helldiver assigned to VB-19 aboard LEXINGTON in August of 1944. The Helldiver, nick-named the 'Beast,' was plagued by numerous technical problems before it began replacing the SBD Dauntless in US Navy dive-bomber squadrons.

Torpedo Squadron Twenty (VT-20) flew this Eastern Aircraft TBM-1C Avenger (133) off LEXINGTON between December of 1944 and late January of 1945. The TBM-1C was the Grumman TBF-1C built under license by Eastern Aircraft.

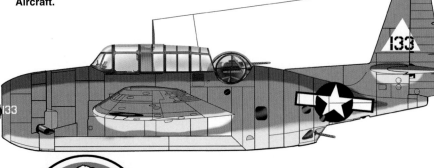

This North American FJ-3M Fury (D-105) was assigned to VF-121 'Pacemakers,' which were embarked on LEXINGTON from April to October of 1957. The Squadron was assigned to Carrier Air Group Twelve (CVG-12) during LEXINGTON's Far East deployment.

Attack Squadron One Ninety Six (VA-196) 'Main Battery' flew this Douglas AD-6 Skyraider (U-413) from LEXINGTON from May until December of 1956. VA-196 was assigned to Air Task Group One (ATG-1) in the Western Pacific.

This Vought F7U-3 Cutlass (U-305, BuNo 129653) was assigned to VA-151 aboard LEXINGTON from May to December of 1956. Engine and mechanical problems caused many Cutlass accidents, which led to its withdrawal from service in 1957.

VF-211 'Flying Checkmates' flew this Grumman F11F-1 Tiger (NP-106, BuNo 141849) from LEXINGTON between April and December of 1959. This cruise with CVG-21 was the only one undertaken with the Tiger aboard this carrier.

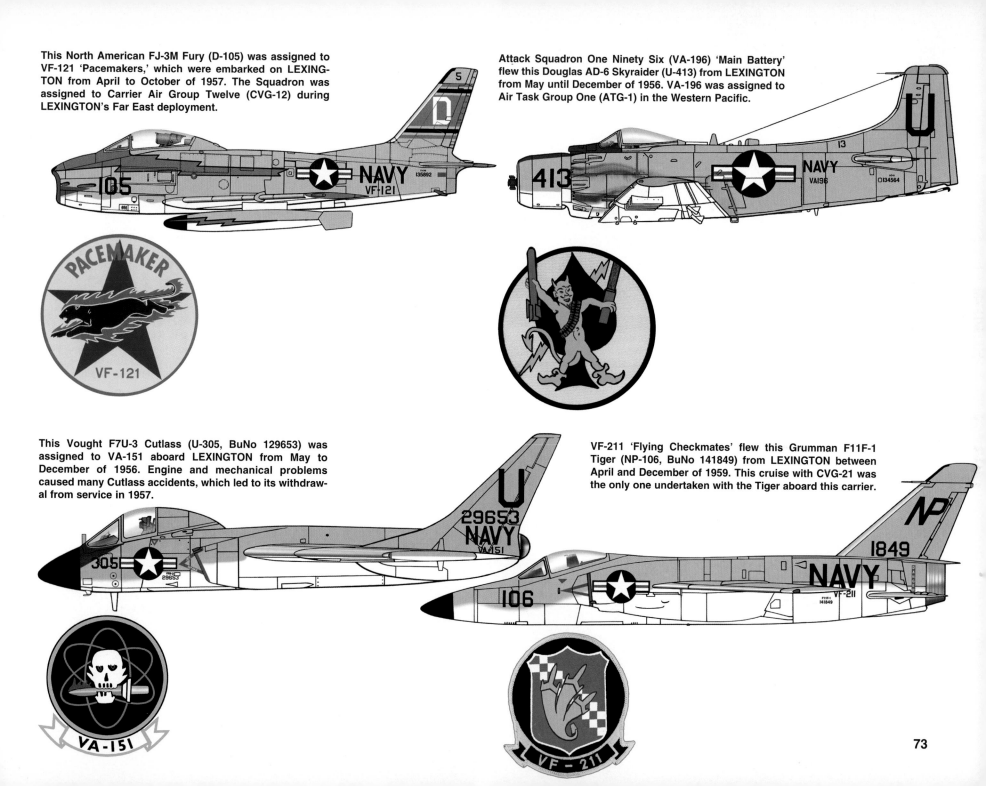

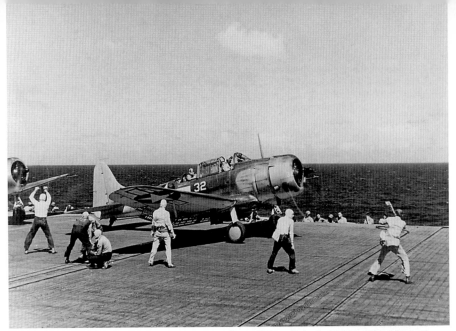

The pilot of this VF-16 F6F-3 Hellcat (32) checks his instruments prior to launching from LEXINGTON in the summer of 1943. The F6F-3 is camouflaged in the tri-color scheme introduced in 1943. The National Insignia has a red surround, which was adopted in June of 1943. VF-16's insignia is painted below the windshield. (The Hook)

LEXINGTON's flight deck officer prepares to flag off the pilot of a VB-16 SBD-5 Dauntless. A 500 pound (226.8 KG) bomb is mounted on the SBD's centerline cradle. The Dauntless served aboard LEXINGTON until replaced by the Curtiss SB2C Helldiver in mid-1944. SBDs were credited with sinking 18 major Japanese warships, including one battleship and six aircraft carriers. (The Hook)

A VB-19 SB2C-4 Helldiver (75) taxis forward on LEXINGTON's flight deck after a bombing mission in the Philippine Islands in August of 1944. The Helldiver collected up a few other nicknames such as 'the Beast' and 'Big Assed Bird.' Pilots liked the SB2C less than the SBD, due to the Helldiver's many mechanical problems and handling difficulties.

A VT-94 Eastern TBM-3E speeds down LEXINGTON's flight deck in 1944. The TBM and the Grumman TBF were identical aircraft built by two different manufacturers. The TBM-3 was used both as a torpedo bomber and as a level bomber carrying up to 2000 pounds (907.2 KG) of bombs. (Grumman)

FJ-3M Furies from VF-121 'Pacesetters' await their turn behind the starboard Jet Blast Deflector (JBD) aboard LEXINGTON in 1957. The FJ-3M was equipped with launching rails on the wings for GAR-8 (later AIM-9) Sidewinder heat seeking air-to-air missiles. Its color scheme was Light Gull Gray (FS36440) over glossy Insignia White (FS17875). The Fury was the navalized version of the Air Force's F-86 Sabre. (The Hook)

An F7U-3 Cutlass is chained to LEXINGTON's deck in 1956. The F7U-3 spent only six months aboard the carrier serving with VA-151, while missile-armed F7U-3Ms of Test Squadron Four (VX-4) were also embarked. The Cutlass suffered many deck crashes and was soon withdrawn from service. The pilots reported cases of nose bleeds climbing the ladder up to the cockpit. (Elsilrac)

A VA-196 AD-6 Skyraider (U-413) has caught the arresting cable and waits for the hook runner to disengage the hook from the 'wire.' This Squadron flew the 'Able Dog' off LEXINGTON from May until December of 1956. The AD was redesignated the A-1 in 1962 to conform to the Military Standard Designations. The Skyraider could carry 15,000 pounds (6804 KG) of ordnance. (Real War Photos)

An F11F-1 Tiger (NP-106, BuNo 141849) taxis forward after recovering on LEXINGTON in 1959. The Tiger was assigned to VF-211, which was part of CVG-21 during this cruise. The F11F's short range resulted in a short service career aboard LEXINGTON and other US carriers. (The Hook)

Training Squadron Five (VT-5) flew this North American T-28C Trojan (2S-708, BuNo 140474) off LEXINGTON in 1965. The T-28C was used for advanced training and carrier qualifications. The Naval Training Command flew the Trojan from 1957 until 1984.

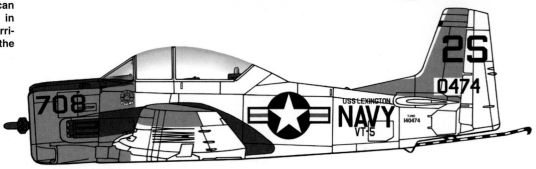

This Grumman F9F-8T Cougar (2N-512, BuNo 146405) was assigned to VT-10 'Cosmic Cats' at NAS Pensacola in the early 1960s. The aircraft (redesignated TF-9J in late 1962) flew in the intermediate flight training role for Naval Flight Officers (NFOs) – the rear seat crews on F-4 Phantom IIs and F-14 Tomcats.

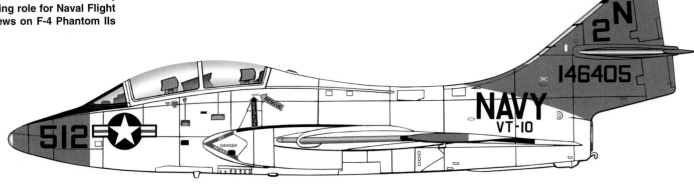

VT-21 'Red Hawks' deployed this TA-4J Skyhawk (A-737) from NAS Kingsville, Texas to LEXINGTON for intermediate and advanced strike training. The TA-4J was based on the earlier TA-4F, but lacked guns and weapons delivery systems.

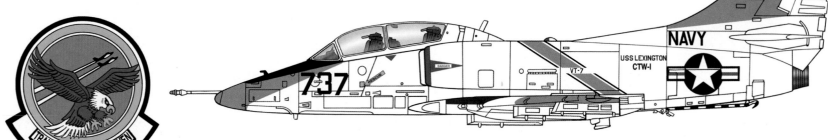

VT-4 'Rubber Ducks' flew this North American T-2C Buckeye (F-817, BuNo 159708) off LEXINGTON. This Pensacola-based Squadron flew basic flight instruction for NFOs and Naval Aviators assigned to the Grumman E-2 Hawkeye and C-2 Greyhound.

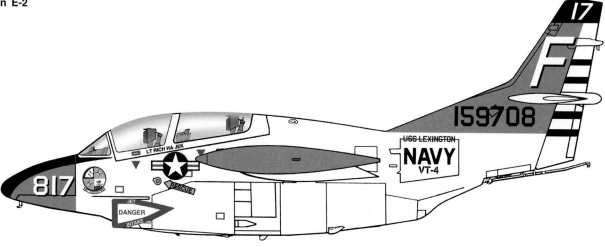

BLUE GHOST #6 was the Grumman C-1A Trader (16, BuNo 146048) which served as LEXINGTON's Carrier Onboard Delivery (COD) aircraft until retired in 1988. The Trader was developed from the S-2 (formerly S2F) Tracker anti-submarine aircraft. It carried up to eight passengers and a crew of three. The nacelle and rudder trim and the title Ghost Riders on the aft nacelle are Insignia Blue (FS15044). (Al Adcock)

Passengers deplane in single file from the C-1A after it landed aboard LEXINGTON. COD passengers wear helmets to protect against injury aboard the aircraft and from noise on the flight deck. The safety crewman guiding the passengers from the Trader wears a white helmet and jersey for easy identification. The C-1A's wings are folded and the aircraft is secured to the flight deck near the port catapult. (Al Adcock)

A VA-113 'Stingers' A-7E Corsair II makes a touch and go approach to LEXINGTON in 1979. The LSO watches for the main gear touchdown location to determine which cable it would have engaged. VA-113 was the West Coast Replacement Air Group (RAG) for A-7Es until decommissioned in 1991. (US Navy)

A US Naval Academy midshipman makes a touch and go landing on LEXINGTON during Flight Orientation in a T-28C Trojan (2S-708, BuNo 140474) in 1965. It was standard procedure to open the canopy of naval aircraft to facilitate escape in the event of a crash. The Trojan was assigned to VT-5 from NAS Saufley Field, a satellite of NAS Pensacola. (The Hook)

Both aircrew climb aboard their A-6E Intruder (NJ-805, BuNo 162188), which is parked on LEXINGTON's Number 3 elevator in September of 1988. The A-6E was assigned to VA-128 'Golden Intruders,' the West Coast Fleet Replenishment Squadron (FRS) from NAS Whidbey Island. This Intruder deployed to LEXINGTON for carrier qualifications. (Al Adcock)

A deck crewman directs a VT-7 TA-4M Skyhawk (A-755) across LEXINGTON's flight deck in 1988. The Skyhawk lacked nose steering, which required use of a nose steering bar on deck. This TA-4M was painted in Marine markings and had a small Soviet-style red star on top of the rudder. (Al Adcock)

LEXINGTON'S Carrier Onboard Delivery (COD) C-1A Trader prepares to engage a cable on landing. The C-1A was used to bring parts and crew from NAS Pensacola to the ship. This aircraft was retired in 1988 and is now displayed at the National Museum of Naval Aviation in Pensacola. An American flag is painted on the C-1A's vertical stabilizer. (Al Adcock)

A Sikorsky SH-3D Sea King (404) hover taxis before receiving the take off order from the Air Boss in LEXINGTON's Pri-Fly in September of 1988. The helicopter was assigned to Helicopter Combat Support Squadron Sixteen (HC-16) 'Bull Frogs' from NAS Pensacola. The SH-3D flew search and rescue missions and barrier patrols to keep civilian vessels from straying into LEXINGTON's path. (Al Adcock)

A VT-7 TA-4J Skyhawk (A-737, BuNo 158513) has its tail hook disengaged by a hook runner onboard LEXINGTON in 1988. VT-7 was assigned to Carrier Training Wing One (CTW-1), which used the TA-4J as an advanced trainer. The two seat Skyhawk saw advanced training service until 1999. (Al Adcock)

A VT-4 T-2C Buckeye (F-817, BuNo 159708) taxis soon after landing aboard LEXINGTON. The Buckeye's pilot is looking toward a Flight Deck Director on the forward deck for directions to his spotting location. VT-4's insignia is painted under the canopy. T-2Cs flew primary and advanced training missions for aviators and NFOs. (Al Adcock)